Bernard Tschumi

Bernard Tschumi

edited by
Giovanni Damiani

Thames & Hudson

Design
Marcello Francone

Architecture Editor
Luca Molinari

Editorial Coordination
Caterina Giavotto

Editing
Gail Ann McDowell
and Lucinda Byatt

*Translation of "Continuity"
by Giovanni Damiani*
Sheila Barker

Layout
Paola Pellegatta

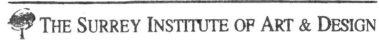
First published in the United Kingdom
in 2003 by Thames & Hudson Ltd,
181A High Holborn, London WC1V 7QX

www.thameshudson.com

British Library Cataloguing-in-Publication Data
A catalogue record for this book is available
from the British Library

ISBN 0-500-28460-1
Printed and bound in Italy

Contents

The Autonomy Effect
K. Michael Hays

Across many of the architectural trends of the past decade—from the new minimalism and "light construction," to the liquid surfaces and blobs generated by high-end media technology, to datascapes and bureaucratic pragmatism—stretches a common interest in the production of effects: the arrangement and distribution of experiential and expressive contents by architectural form. The range of this interest extends from carefully fabricated construction details and attention to the surfaces of materials, intended to coax out the latent sensuous qualities and moods of a building, to complex, large-scale formal and programmatic systems and various "soft infrastructures" that attempt to engineer and manage effects through new forms of advertising and distribution of information, graphics and software.

If the common interest is the production of effects, the issue that has been roundly dismissed from contemporary architecture discourse is architecture's autonomy. For the autonomy thesis as it was widely discussed in the 1970s involved a constellation of now suspect concepts including architecture's legibility, its irreducibility (that is, the fact that the "meaning" of architectural form exceeds any quantifiable program or set of behaviors as well as technological determinants), disciplinary specificity, and "criticality"—the last of which involves architecture's ability to resist and negate the consumer culture that surrounds it. Recent design theories have tended rather to take an affirmative position with regard to their cultural sponsors, blurring disciplinary boundaries in an effort to expand into new markets, and seem to have accepted a certain determination of architecture by the new media apparatus and demands for consumption against which, it is assumed, architecture can no longer gain purchase. Architectural autonomy, by the lights of the current discourse, seems not only retrograde as an idea but obstructive as an ideal.

What I want to propose here is that the recent turn toward the production of effects, which seems to be directly opposed to the earlier autonomy project, is, in fact, an outcome of the autonomy project—not that the recent positions arose like a phoenix from the ash heap of that project's failure, but that the issue of effects was implied in the autonomy thesis all along, was an always-latent potentiality and a necessary outcome of following a project through to its logical conclusion. Even so, this outcome is not a matter of logic alone, but rather of a specific history and unfolding of architectural concepts that I will attempt to sketch out briefly here. At the center of that history is the work of Bernard Tschumi.

1. A set of essays written by Tschumi in 1975-76 is, in part, his taking account of the current state of architectural discourse, staking out a ter-

Alfred Lerner
Hall Student Center,
Columbia University

ritory in the field that he believes he can occupy productively. In particular, the essays are a meditation on the opposition between architecture as a product of the mind, a conceptual and dematerialized discipline, and architecture as the sensual experience of space and a spatial praxis. In the earliest of the essays, "Questions of Space: The Pyramid and the Labyrinth (or the Architectural Paradox)," Tschumi formulates the autonomy thesis first in Hegelian terms: as an image of the *Geist*'s progressive attempts to overcome matter, architecture is by its nature involved with building but not reducible to building. (Think of the ancient pyramids as proclaiming or symbolizing the presence of an inner entity, a spirit and concept, to which their built form is manifestly extrinsic.) Architecture is an "artistic supplement," a set of concepts added to building. Or conversely, as Tschumi puts it, the "function and technical characteristics of a house or a temple [are] the means to an end that excludes those very characteristics." By 1975 we could recognize that architecture is, above all, the production of concepts and, with that, the paradox that "the architect could finally achieve the sensual satisfaction that the making of material objects no longer provided."[1]

While such a post-functionalist, pro-conceptual declamation captures the prevalent mood of progressive architecture in the mid-1970s (one could compare similar statements by Peter Eisenman, Diana Agrest, and others), Tschumi moves through his analysis to a more distinctive conclusion. First, he poses the ideological dilemma of the autonomy project (which he seems almost alone in recognizing), namely, "If the architectural piece renounces its autonomy by recognizing its latent ideological and financial dependency, it accepts the mechanisms of society. If it sanctuarizes itself in an art-for-art's-sake position, it does not escape classification among existing ideological compartments."[2] Even the utopian energies of the radical architectures of the 1960s, with which Tschumi clearly sympathizes, eventually devolve into a "desperate attempt" to deconceal the materials and forces of ideology, "ironically verifying where the system was going," and thus becoming (merely) ideological themselves. By the time of Tschumi's writing, "architecture seemed to have gained autonomy by opposing the institutional framework. But in the process it had become the institutional opposition, thus growing into everything it tried to oppose."[3]

Tschumi then meets this ideological dilemma with an Adorno-like strategy of negation: "So architecture seems to survive only when it saves its nature by negating the form that society expects of it. I would therefore suggest that there has never been any reason to doubt the necessity of architecture, for the necessity of architecture is its non-necessity. It is useless but radically so." According to Tschumi, there is no avant-garde that is not enabled, but also contained, by what it opposes. Architecture's autonomy allows it to stand against the very social order with which it is complicit, yet the same complicity racks architecture into an agonistic position—combative, transgressive, striving to produce effects that are of the system yet against the system. The possibility is long past to prescribe normality for architecture, either in terms of function or performance, or of cultural representation or social service. We must now see the conflicts and discontents of a discipline and a practice that, in order to have a vocation at all in the cultural world, must unflinchingly refuse to conform to expectations. Finally, he announces his conclusion with all the force of historical inevitability: "This means, in effect, that, perhaps for the first time in history, architecture can never be... The only alternative to the paradox is silence, a final nihilistic statement that might provide modern architectural history with its ultimate punchline, its self-annihilation."[4]

That architecture, since it clearly had a beginning, might conceivably also have an end, is easy enough to conceptualize in the Hegelian scheme of things (we owe the original end-of-art thesis to Hegel, after all), all the more so after "the sixties," when we began to know something of the profound complicity of cultural institutions and university systems, not to mention the building and development industries, with state power and the perpetuation of the status quo. But Tschumi's meditations on the Hegelian supplement, it seems to me, are less motivated by the 1960s end-of-art debate, already well rehearsed if not over by 1975, than by a dawning awareness of the particular historical fatedness of architecture itself, of a specific cultural production—perhaps the most deeply social of all—now inevitably suffering its own unique, historically determined recontainment, reterritorialization, and implosion after more than two centuries of opening, transgression, and revolt. By 1975—in the face of a devastating economic recession, the first energy crisis, as well as the weariness of the Vietnam war—architecture's immanent end had become perhaps less a matter of willful self-annihilation than a far less spectacular fading away of its comparative social relevance. What is more, the discourse of autonomy in its weaker, reductive forms seemed to reduce architecture to the mere availability of preexisting elements and combinatory techniques from some virtual stock, to an operator of formal possibilities with no further potential for engagement. For Tschumi, the logic of the autonomy project thus proves that winners lose; so architectural autonomy must itself be volatilized.

To this end, in the last sections of the essay, Tschumi offers a brief, tentative mention of a possible alternative to self-annihilation and silence, one that might accelerate and intensify architecture's paradox rather than relieve it: he calls it "experienced space," which, more than a perception or a concept of space, is a process, a way of practicing space, an *event*. The term was, of course, a highly charged one for Tschumi; it represented a reversal of the object-subject hierarchy of the 1970s neo-avant-garde, and it was related both to the situationists' *événement* ("whose symbolic and exemplary value lay in their seizure of urban space and not in the design of what was built") and to Bataille's *expérience intérieure*—two of Tschumi's emotional and intellectual role models that were largely unconsidered at the time. Tschumi later illustrated the notion of an event with examples of "cross-programming" like pole-vaulting in a cathedral, bicycling in the laundromat, sky diving in the elevator shaft. What is important for us here is that, for Tschumi, an architecture of events appears dialectically as a possible third term between the contradiction of autonomy and negation; it is of both autonomy and negation and, indeed, should reveal the productivity of the contradiction even as it dissolves the contradiction. It is that revelation (perhaps it is not too strong a word) that is announced in the early essays and that Tschumi's subsequent work must enact. It is the story of that enactment that I must now begin to tell.

2. At the same time Tschumi was writing "The Architectural Paradox," he was also working on his *Advertisements for Architecture*, a series of architectural montages, two of which featured photographs of the Villa Savoye he had taken in 1965 while a student at the ETH, where he found "the squalid walls of the small service rooms on the ground floor, stinking of urine, smeared with excrement, and covered with obscene graffiti." How should we read these *Advertisements*? When they have been read at all, they have been seen as an explicit alternative to the over-privileging of pure, autonomous form by Aldo Rossi, Peter Eisenman, and others (already known as the "Whites") and to Colin Rowe's influential preference for the uncorrupted, pristine flesh of Le Corbusier. Surely this reading is correct as far as it goes: Tschumi's "Architecture and Transgression," the text that accompanied the publication of the *Advertisements* in *Oppositions* 7, 1976, returns to the themes of "The Architectural Paradox" and reintroduces the transgressive eroticism of Georges Bataille explicitly against his contemporary, Le Corbusier. "The contradiction between architectural concept and the sensual experience of space resolves itself at one point of tangency: *the rotten point*, the very point that taboos and culture have always rejected."[5] But Tschumi elsewhere augments this, describing the *Advertisements* in a slightly different way, as a notational device to "trigger" the desire for architecture, and not an architecture of autonomy and negation, but of perverse pleasure. Stressing the inevitable commodification of architecture, he queries the possibility of accelerating rather than resisting that logic into an erotics of architecture. Tschumi writes, "The usual function of advertisements... is to trigger desire for something beyond the [image or form] itself. As there are advertisements for products, why not advertisements for architecture?" But this is advertising in libidinal terms—intensities, perversions, and violence—following, no doubt, Baitaille, but also the advertisements for art by Ed Ruscha in California and J. G. Ballard in Paris, both of which pushed art through the channels of commodity distribution in order to dialectically escape the market itself, and both of which Tschumi is surely nodding to in his title, *Advertisements*.

By replacing conventional architectural drawings with notational systems (here photographs and texts) that trigger or evoke or mark a possible architectural experience, the *Advertisements for Architecture* throw into difficulty the sorting through of the relays among author, object, performance, audience, and so forth. (For example, is the author here Tschumi, Le Corbusier, or those who smeared the excrement? Is the architectural content already present before the photograph that reduplicates it, or is content only there in the combination of photograph and text? Or is it not there at all until produced by a specific reader, and then only in the mind of that particular reader?) Tschumi's attempt seems to establish architectural notation as an autonomous process of graphic and textual production that is not secondary to some building it denotes (as are conventional architectural drawings) but also has no predetermined relationship to the spatial performance it solicits or triggers. The notational system simply marks or frames a generalized architectural potential, an enabling condition comprising a derivation (Le Corbusier's villa) and distortion (the photograph of its squalid condition), an augmentation (the captions), but also, importantly, a gap, a desire that must be filled or performed by each reader of these works. Not architecture itself is offered, Adorno might say, but only evidence that it exists—exists as an event, exists in its concept and its effects, which are nevertheless every bit as material as "the real thing."

Let me try to unpack this a bit and relate it back to the theme of autonomy from which we began. Tschumi is banking here on the main argument of the autonomy thesis: the production of architecture results from a labor of a very specific and precise sort whose enabling conditions preexist any particular architectural project. The designer does not fabricate the materials he works with; the materials of architectural practice are not neutral and thereby available to a unity that is imposed upon them by the architect. (This is why, according to the thesis, it is a mystification to speak of the architect as a genius or a creator.)

It is rather that the materials of architecture, its elements and operations, possess and preserve a specific weight and formative potential of their own that, while creating conditions for elaboration and expansion, more emphatically demand constraint and conservation. Architectural decisions are already determined by the discourse itself; the architect neither invents nor chooses them. The architect discovers rather than creates the project, encounters experiences rather than devises solutions. Therefore, in a certain sense, if the architectural system is autonomous, there is nothing that can be added to it, notwithstanding the illusion of choice, and nothing to do but continue it in the hope that the product of continuance will be an increase in experience and understanding.

At the same time, however, there is the haunting resonance that the whole thing could have been set up differently, that the entire architectural system and its authority is a fragile artifice. But then, rather than free the practice of architecture from its own autonomy, this arbitrariness, on the contrary, further enforces the constraints of autonomy, in the sense that its necessity is not derived from the real but rather from a fiction added to it, not a raw material but a product that, as such, must constantly be produced. Through a kind of *Nachträglichkeit*, architecture is constantly retraced and rehearsed, though never really present as an unproblematic *donnée*.[6] Architecture must constantly be produced, or better, repeated, *as architecture*.

By defining architecture as a repetition born of very precise beginnings and enabling conditions, on the one hand, and a performance and production of unprecedented desires and experiences, on the other, in these early works Tschumi initiated a crisis but also a potential in architecture that has been barely acknowledged, even as subsequent developments up to our own present seem to fulfill his predictions. Indeed, his particular differentiation of architecture from its medium, made in these early essays and conceptual projects, will later be developed to eventually mark the extreme limits of the Hegelian supplement, which is to say, of autonomy as such, turning it into what we now perceive, according to contemporary theoretical discourse, as its very opposite, the production of effects. But in Tschumi's work, beginning as early as 1975, it is as if through a rigorous pursuit of autonomy, we have already tunneled through to the other side, the side of effects (like the electron in quantum theory that is on both sides of a barrier at the same time), finding within the autonomy project a practice that tries to keep faith with some more fundamental state of contingency or meaninglessness, with a delirium and euphoria of repetition rather than either an affirmation of form or a melancholy of loss. In 1975-76 Tschumi announced what would become the legacy of the most advanced of contemporary practice: architecture can maintain itself *in effect* even as the moment to realize it in actuality has passed, and, equally perhaps, has not yet come again.

3. *The Manhattan Transcripts* (1976-81) pushes this research further into an architecture of the event and effect. The city of Manhattan, rather than the Villa Savoye, is now the cathexis-object, a city understood as having an erotic and violent programmatic potential woven into its grid of streets and avenues. The *Transcripts* are presented in three horizontal banded diagrams: the photographic fragment now acts as a metaphor for the architectural program—a murder in Central Park and the flight of the fugitive to the simulated pleasures of pornography and prostitution on 42nd Street. The architectural drawings are distortions of traditional cities and gardens. The fugitive's flight is traced in a choreographic notation of lines and arrows, tracing movements and interactions. These three notational bands produce aleatory interactions both horizontally and vertically in the same way that the street grid and buildings of Manhattan do, but in perhaps an even more multidimensional and heterogeneous space in which a variety of significations, constructed and appropriated, interact, blend, and clash.

It is in the project for the Parc de la Villette of 1982-83 where the attempt, begun almost a decade earlier, to produce the concept and the experience of architecture by blocking its actual manifestation achieves its final limit condition. For the "trigger" that would produce architectural desire has now been reduced to a grid of thirty points superimposed by two kinds of lines, intersecting and meandering, in a deployment of analytic elements so visually reduced and incomplete to eyes still trained for form and habituated to fuller kinds of visual language, that they, indeed, might not be counted as architecture at all. The project is more like a kind of architectural DNA: all of the information necessary for the generation of a fully functioning programmatic-spatial organism is present in its geometric encoding, but none of the substance. *La Case Vide*, Tschumi named the project: the empty square, the marker or place holder for the events to come; not a pure, autonomous architecture but an architecture of pure event, architecture that asserts itself as something emergent rather than final, something that we have to strain to keep in focus and, even then, only momentarily, just before it slips out of our perception and in the next instant is already lost—architecture as autonomy effect.

No one understood this more than Jacques Derrida. What Derrida called his own double writing (*écriture double*) provokes, on the one hand, an inversion of the general cultural domination he everywhere identifies with Western metaphysics and the history of Western philosophy, and enacts, on the other hand, a new text that, necessarily, participates in the very principles it deconstructs, but participates as an invasion and a volatilization, releasing the dissonance of the inherited order. In his 1986 essay on *La Case Vide*, Derrida finds in Tschumi's project an architecture of the same formulation: *l'architecture double*, an architecture of absolute autonomy together with absolute negation, an architecture of event, what I have called the autonomy effect. Derrida characteristically sees this architecture as a play of differences and traces of differences, as a "spacing," or a "production of intervals without which the 'full' terms would not signify, would not function."[7] And he makes the important point that among the excesses that burst through what appears, at first gloss, to be only the effacement of architecture, are parallel systems of the same sort Tschumi earlier invoked in *The Manhattan Transcripts*—photography, cinematography, choreography—all of which are here, in the La Villette project, grafted onto the points, lines, and surfaces as a kind of hypertext. Before the availability of the multi-media technology that would literally dissolve architecture into other media forms, the La Villette project finds the multimedia conceptual apparatus that architecture produces in its own self-definition. Tschumi's fireworks of 1992 at the realized park offered, alternatively, a spectacle of pure performance as such, completing the dyad of trigger and effect that the *Advertisements* first announced.

All of Tschumi's later works follow from and develop these projects. For example, if *The Manhattan Transcripts* remain in the category of architectural research, the Tokyo Opera, 1986, carries that research to a full-blown building proposal. The notational bands are now transformed into built spaces that choreograph the same sort of intense *différance* or heterogeneity of events that the *Transcripts* record—a "hypermetropolitan stage," Tschumi calls it, a *dispositif* or distribution apparatus made up of an absolute minimum of form to generate a maximum of spontaneous events. In a similar transformation, Le Fresnoy National Studio for Contemporary Arts in Tourcoing takes the notion of interval or spacing developed in La Villette and now finds its surrealist potential in a strategy of the in-between. Robert Somol has likened the juxtaposition of the new steel roof and the old tile-roofed sheds to Breton's canonic umbrella and sewing machine on the operating table, "the crossing of an existing building fabric of material decay and disuse with a highly technologically and media-driven piece of infrastructural support (the roof as umbrella)," while Tschumi himself mentions its relation to Frederick Kiesler's surrealist multimedia theater projects of the 1920s and 30s.[8] But again, Tschumi's project is a machine for effect with built form deployed, it seems, almost reluctantly, and then as efficiently, minimally, and non-rhetorically as possible. For the desired effect of semiotic flux and radical connectivity cannot be accomplished with forms laden with traditional meaning. Surrealism conjoined with *Sachlichkeit*, then, for the eroticism of decay that was first announced in the *Advertisements* is now actualized in the blunt appropriation of a found object, the existing, hollowed-out old sheds—an operation that abolishes even the illusion of autonomy and dissolves the project back into a materialism and a corporeality that Tschumi had sought since the early essays.

4. I have claimed that the reversal of architecture understood as autonomous formal operations and architecture understood as the diagrammatic production of effects was theorized by Tschumi as early as 1975 and was played out in his work in a dialectical process over the subsequent years. But the real significance of Tschumi's work (at least for this historian) will not be grasped fully until we can take a further step and restore the social and historical meaning of this reversal by positing it as a trace and an abstraction from a specific historical problem. I am not able to complete that project here but, by way of conclusion, I would like to suggest a provisional way of preparing to map Tschumi's conceptual project onto the more general socio-cultural context.

Most generally, the essays, the *Advertisements*, and the later projects that I see as developing their preliminary theses, should be seen as progressive attempts to find architectural examples of the kind of text analyzed by Roland Barthes as an intransitive, performative writing, a textuality in which the very autonomy of the text assures that reading it, performing it, is an activity of production in its own right. Barthes himself understood this text as historically determined, as a response to a situation in which the failed past must be rejected but a future was not yet even on the horizon. In his 1973 *Le Plaisir du Texte*, Barthes makes the now famous formulation of *plaisir* and *jouissance*, which first opposes and then joins the two types of pleasure, and coordinates binaries like art's conformist disciplinary constraints as against its revolutionary political potentials, its conceptual rigor as against its sensuality, its closed and open processes of signification, and even our present dialectic of autonomy and effect. Barthes:

Text of pleasure [*texte de plaisir*]: the text that contents, fills, grants euphoria; the text that comes from culture and does not break with it, is linked to a *comfortable* practice of reading. Text of bliss [*texte de jouissance*]: the text that imposes a state of loss, the text that discomforts (perhaps to the point of a certain boredom), unsettles the reader's historical, cultural, psychological assumptions, the consistency of his tastes, values, memories, brings to a crisis his relation with language.[9]

But Barthes's point is not merely to invade the proper with the improper but to recognize the "anachronic" processes *before* their separation:

Now the subject who keeps the two texts in his field and in his hands the reins of pleasure and bliss is an anachronic subject, for he simultaneously and contradictorily participates in the profound hedonism of all culture [...] and in the destruction of that culture: he enjoys the consistency of his selfhood (that is his pleasure) and seeks its loss (that is his bliss). He is a subject split twice over, doubly perverse.[10]

Tschumi's entire career can be seen, in a certain sense, as an ongoing attempt to enact this simultaneous distinction and combination on an architectural terrain. His own *texte de plaisir*—the references to the canonic "texts" such as the Villa Savoye, Manhattan, nineteenth-century gardens, and Constructivism, to name just a few—promotes a self-conscious, reflected appreciation within a bounded inventory of entities, techniques, and evaluative categories of the architectural discipline. *Plaisir* pertains to the propriety, comfort, and security of historical knowledge; *plaisir* figures as the premature normality of architecture that Tschumi sought to overthrow. On the other hand, Tschumi's *texte de jouissance*—enacted by the techniques of montage, juxtaposition, trace, appropriation, in general, by the volatilization, distortion, and evacuation of the canonic material—cuts the viewer adrift from these standard topoi of architecture culture, unanchors fixed expectations about architecture. *Jouissance*, in Tschumi's work, results from a kind of surrender to the desultory forces of history that he charted in the early essays (and includes a kind of dialectical flirtation with the consumerism, technological positivism, and experiential nominalism that are the latest external "threats" to architecture)—from some readiness to yield, to submerge, to sink below architecture's deceptively ordered surfaces into the very disjointed, decentered experiences that a more "proper" architecture would try to escape. The *texte de jouissance* takes erotic pleasure in accomplishing the death of its subject which, as we have seen, is nothing less than architecture itself.

What must be insisted upon is that this architectural *jouissance* is impossible to read except as a historical response to a dilemma of architecture (the ideological dilemma first announced in Tschumi's early writings, which recently has become only more exacerbated), indeed, the end of architecture that he perversely welcomed, made from the divided consciousness of a cultural producer and an intellectual who desired a social relevance that society itself denied him. (Recall, "the necessity of architecture is its non-necessity.") An earlier generation of architects who experienced the same dilemma—I have in mind, for example, Peter Eisenman, Aldo Rossi, and in a certain sense, John Hejduk—often responded to the situation in the different register of the absurd. The motif of the absurd defines the existential side of the historical problem—the practical impossibility of making meaning in a meaningless world—and the autonomy thesis appeared in that register, as often as not, as an architecture of melancholy and despair. But for Tschumi, the post-existentialist, post-structuralist architect *par excellence*, meaning was never seen as an idealized goal, a hoped-for-even-if-impossible endpoint, but rather as a blockage and a closure within an exhausted discipline. The transit of the autonomy question between these two generations is best grasped, then, as a passage from the absurd to *jouissance*, which must be understood as two different models that try to manage the same historical situation. And the autonomy effect, whose history I have tried to sketch out here, is the architectural legacy of that situation in our own time.

[1] Bernard Tschumi, "The Architectural Paradox," in *Architecture and Disjunction*, MIT Press, Cambridge, MA 1996 p. 32.

[2] *Ibid.*, p. 46.

[3] *Ibid.*, p. 45.

[4] *Ibid.*, p. 48.

[5] Bernard Tschumi, "Architecture and Transgression," in *Architecture and Disjunction*, p. 76.

[6] According to the Freudian theory of *Nachträglichkeit* or deferred action, precocious sexual stimulation normally has no psychopathological repercussions at the time of its occurrence, due to the child's psychical incapacity to comprehend the act of seduction. With the physiological change of puberty, however, the mnemic-psychical trace—inscribed in the unconcious as if in an unknown language—would be transformed (rewritten, reiterated) as trauma and displaced as symptom in neurosis.

[7] Jacques Derrida, *Positions*, trans. Alan Bass, University of Chicago Press, Chicago, IL 1981, p. 27.

[8] R.E. Somol, "In Form Falls Fiction. Misreading the Avantgarde in Contemporary Architecture," unpublished manuscript (1997), p. 206. Bernard Tschumi, *Event-Cities (Praxis)*, MIT Press, Cambridge, MA 1994, p. 399.

[9] Roland Barthes, *The Pleasure of the Text*, trans. Richard Miller, Hill and Wang, New York 1975, p. 14.

[10] *Ibid.*

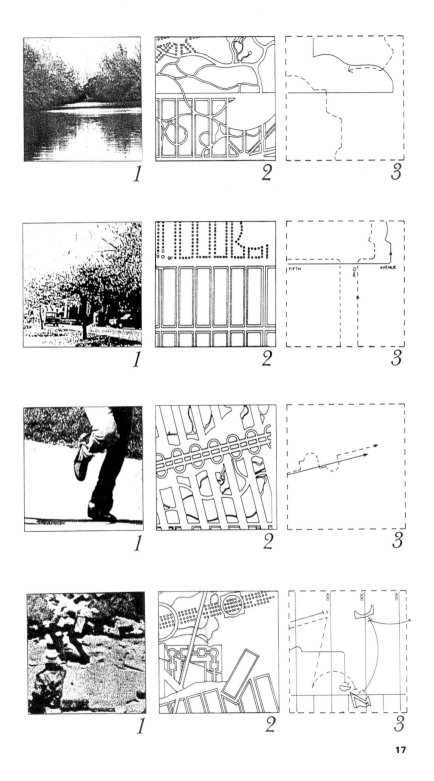

1   2   3

1   2   3

1   2   3

1   2   3

Intertextuality
Interview with Marco De Michelis

MDM: *I would first like to discuss the question of space. In your first article in 1975, you began a discourse on space, which you defined as an essential element of architecture. But your definition of space is complex— it isn't space as a geometrical element but rather as it is connected with use, movement, and dynamics. Are you still interested in this question today?*

BT: Yes, of course. At the time, it was necessary to define architecture outside of its historical determination, and I was trying to find a "detour" or device to approach it. Instead of talking about form or typologies, I was looking for other constituents—space, movement, use; concepts that were removed from cultural and historical determination and had been ignored by the dominant history of architecture as form. Today, I am still trying to do that, knowing that it is ultimately impossible, because you are always somehow confronted with the materiality of a building.

MDM: *I recognize some historical origins in your attitude. For example, when you went to London in 1970, Cedric Price's* Fun Palace *represented a new notion of an architectural space as an organization of movements and events.*

BT: As a student, I was interested in Cedric's work, and the reason was that I was discovering that you could devise an architecture without actually being "architectural." You could build with concepts, designing the conditions for architecture rather than conditioning designs. During this period I was also quite aware of some of the Archizoom projects like the *No Stop City* because they were introducing a different cultural and political agenda. They were trying to "verify where the system was going" by taking specific conceptual themes to an extreme.

MDM: *I have a second question about space, which always becomes a part of life if a human body moves inside of it. Your insight pertains to a German tradition, a genealogy of spatial thought that seems to have been interrupted. Architectural history was born as a science with notions like the psychology of architecture and the sensation of space, but nobody speaks about these issues today.*

BT: This is quite intriguing because, indeed, the question is hardly raised today; we increasingly belong to a culture of images that need to be reproduced on television or through the media. These are always identifiable images of a certain sort, and little that has to do with the sensation of space, or with the multiple interpretations that space can carry

19

depending on what happens in it. Because these concepts of what happens in space are hard to communicate through the mass media, they tend to disappear outside of the general discourse. In other words, the discourse of space still exists, but in a position that is somewhat marginal to the discourse of architectural surfaces or visual forms.

MDM: *Do you think we somehow lack the words to speak about space?*
BT: Well, I think the problem is that the real discourse of space has been replaced by the discourse of the surface which, as I said, interests me less than the social or programmatic dimensions of what happens inside. I tend, however, to be interested in the notion of the "envelope," because of a certain logic that says that if you want to define spaces, you have to work with envelopes, with the material that contains or "envelopes" them.

MDM: *Envelope is a key word. At Le Fresnoy, you made a kind of scaffold building: You have the big roof, the stairs, and the walkways. The big roof is a cover generating interstitial spaces….*
BT: Le Fresnoy was our first building in the envelope discussion. It is also about absolute heterogeneity in that this new facility for multimedia crossovers involved multiple programs—music, film, and television studios, production and exhibition spaces, cafés, a library, lodging, performance spaces—and the umbrella of the great roof provided a kind of "common denominator" for this diversity. The roof also provided an envelope for the different existing buildings from the 1920s amusement facility that we had been asked to demolish, but decided to keep. This heterogeneity of programs and spaces was an "*objet trouvé*," or found object, that we decided to play or work with in our strategy for the project.
In more recent work, the client's program is often more homogeneous, and therefore the interpretation of the notion of the envelope is quite different. For example, at Rouen, the program is a large concert hall, and there are two separate material envelopes with circulation between them. Heterogeneity returns in a moment of transgression or interference, such as in the movements of crowds through the building.

MDM: *The mission of the historical avant-garde of the beginning of the 20th century was to bring art into life and to merge art and architecture. The polarisation between the two was the mental figure of modernism; modernity meant polarisation, division, opposition.*
Do you think that we are still looking for a solution to the merging of art into life?
BT: I don't think the problem is the same today because our media culture has eroded the boundary between art and life. Everything has sort of become a common denominator of modern communication. In my own work, I try to reintroduce certain oppositions or conflicting relationships between two or three terms, for example, in juxtaposing the continuity of the envelope to the discontinuity of events so as to re-establish dynamic oppositions or conflicts.

MDM: *All these questions are followed by one that I think is crucial: If space as movement, time, and flux, is architecture, doesn't this mean that the notion of tectonics is definitively dead?*

BT: Yes, materiality is alive but tectonics are dead.

MDM: *In 1913, one of my favourite architects from the early 20th century, Rudolph Schindler, said that if architectural space becomes a key question of architecture, it's the end of an architecture conceived of as construction. He said that he would not build to support a roof, but rather as an artist to produce a space. This begs the question of what architecture actually is. You once wrote about Hegel's famous artistic supplement, meaning that architecture is the supplement a building has over its utilitarian function. What actually is the supplement?*

BT: Before we get to the supplement, let's go back to Schindler's notion of the roof. As we know, the roof at the beginning of the 20th century was already purely a cultural artefact. You already had Frederic Kiesler's house where there was no distinction between the wall and the roof; to define "the roof," "the door," or "the window" was in a way to remain within a very specific ontology. This, of course, brings difficulties. And this is where the discussion on the supplement becomes interesting, considering that without the supplement, there really is no "architecture" in a cultural sense. As architects, we are all endlessly developing a discourse on the supplement. As I said earlier, if architecture could get away from the supplement, it would always be brought back simply to those constituent elements—movement, space, and the social activities or events that happen within space.

MDM: *Architects at the end of the 1960s and the beginning of the 1970s like Aldo Rossi thought of architecture as an autonomous discipline with its own typology and morphology, and as a tool to interpret the complexity of the world. You have said that architecture needs to import and export from other fields, suggesting that is an open rather than a closed form of knowledge. Does architecture then produce knowledge, and is it a productive action?*

BT: To answer your first question, I would say that architecture isn't any different from mathematics, physics, art, or literature in that it is constantly producing knowledge. Again, just as in physics or mathematics, certain concepts sometimes can be "exported" into other disciplines and instrumentalized. To answer the second: While the making of architecture is a productive action, the building is a productive action not in itself but rather as something that will create conditions of use. It is only through the conditions of use that something can be produced, hence the question of autonomy cannot exist without the question of what might be called architecture's "intertextuality." For me, the object of architecture does not exist as "architecture." The object of architecture is always corrupted by its use.

MDM: *Speaking of intertextuality, you often suggest analogies between architecture and art or film.*

BT: People use analogies all of the time because it's often the simplest way to explain things. Every now and then, however, it is more strategic. For example, I have taken certain concepts like montage or ideas of sequence from film because they could tell me something about architecture. They provided a set of tools, a theoretical tool. Historically, the theory of architecture has dealt with facades, tectonics, and so forth, but the constructs that I needed in order to discuss certain architectural interests didn't exist within the discipline of architecture. This analogical way of thinking is comparable to Durand's looks at the natural sciences, the concept of the organic, and scientific modes of classification in his architectural treatises. He, too, was looking for tools to help him think through questions of architecture.

MDM: *That brings me to notation, which is very interesting for architecture and crucial to your generation. Plans, sections, and elevations are not enough to describe your design process. Daniel Libeskind has described drawing as more than the reduction inside of a orthogonal grid of the complexity of architectural thinking. Some of your early drawings bring to mind choreographer's notations.*

BT: The notation systems of dancers and athletes, such as the football players in *The Manhattan Transcripts*, interested me because they allowed me to address certain architectural concerns that could not be expressed in plans, sections, or elevations, namely, dynamic movements that take place in time. One of the most extreme examples in my work occurred when I was asked to design fireworks for the opening of La Villette. I worked with firework manufacturers, who did not seem to have a notation system, so I tried to invent a mode of notation that would introduce specific issues of time and movement into the fireworks display. One advantage of using notations from fields outside of architecture is that they have not been solidified into codes in the way that plans, sections, and elevations have. They thus provide a good means of developing concepts. Unfortunately, however, you have to translate back into the general architectural code later on at a different state of development, so that these concepts can be understood within the building industry.

MDM: *The topics of intertextuality and notation bring up the question of the hybridization of architecture. A question that has been discussed for the last twenty years is the question of the relationships between architecture and the other arts, and between individual architects and visual artists. Do you see the relationships as having changed over the last two or three decades?*

BT: If I look back at the 1970s, I think that a key moment existed when some of the issues that were raised in conceptual or performance art were directly relevant to the explorations of certain architects. Many of these issues, which concerned activating or defining physical spaces, have been either resolved or abandoned. Today, in a very different way that is largely impelled by our electronic environment, the two disciplines are coming together again in a common body of work on the surface or image.

A number of video and installation artists are questioning the relationship between the real and the virtual, or using media or moving images as means to define spaces in ways that parallel architects' uses of virtual spaces as a viable component of architecture. From screens defining architectural spaces to the kind of virtual urban world that we see today in Times Square, you find areas opened by the digital environment that are equally explored by artists and architects.

MDM: *There is a beautiful quotation by the French philosopher Paul Ricoeur in which he discusses the possibility of a narrative structure in architecture and says that built space is "condensed time." You speak about sequences and about analogies with film. Do you think that architectural space can have a narrative structure?*

BT: I am very suspicious of the idea that architecture tells a story, or that it can be used to tell the story of institutions. I remember an important text by Roland Barthes on the structural analysis of narratives in which he deconstructed the notion of narrative by emphasizing the structural components; hence you find out that the components of the narration are interchangeable or, in other words, are not pre-determined. If you apply endless permutation or recombination to narrative, the narrative becomes, how can I say, "aleatory narrative." I think it is important to stress that architectural narrative should never be addressed in a linear fashion. As we perceive or experience them, the series of fragments that make up architecture are constantly rearranging in different ways, so that there is no single linear path, even though one of the favourite means of architectural organization is linear. The structure of the narrative is not populated by a single story, but by many stories, or rather, by different stories for different people. Architecture never conveys a singular story.

MDM: *Do you think that the design process can be conceived of as a series of transformations, transmutations, and manipulations?*

BT: Yes, I do, but with an immediate qualification: Architecture does not need many permutations, because architecture is much simpler than verbal language. As a result, architecture doesn't need to get into the level of complexity of language, or it gets lost in a nightmare. One reason, of course, is that words are cheap and fast while architecture is expensive and time-consuming. To put it another way, architecture carries a critical mass. When you start to build, constraints allow only certain permutations to make sense, as opposed to language, where permutations are almost endless. To return to the idea of architectonic: tectonics used to indicate that only one type of hierarchical organization was correct; we know that this is not true, but we also know that certain ways or manipulations quickly become *"un jeu de l'esprit,"* a gratuitous game of the mind. Also, and quite specifically, the construction industry has its own logic, and you always play both with and against that logic. To follow this line of thinking: the idea that, for example, a structure can pervert or question the idea of the envelope is something that interests me. As we talk, I'm thinking of a project that we currently are designing for the

University of Cincinnati in Cincinnati, Ohio. It doesn't have a front or a back; it doesn't have a corner, and the structure that supports it is also a façade. Sometimes it's "structure"; sometimes it's not. I can bring back nearly every one of the questions we discussed today to this real, practical object. This includes questions about the narrative and the linear. I feel that increasingly we are trying to challenge the received definitions of architecture, but doing it in terms of the forces of construction. Once again, I would like to say that architecture is not about forms, but about forces.

Le Fresnoy National Studio
for the Contemporary Arts,
model

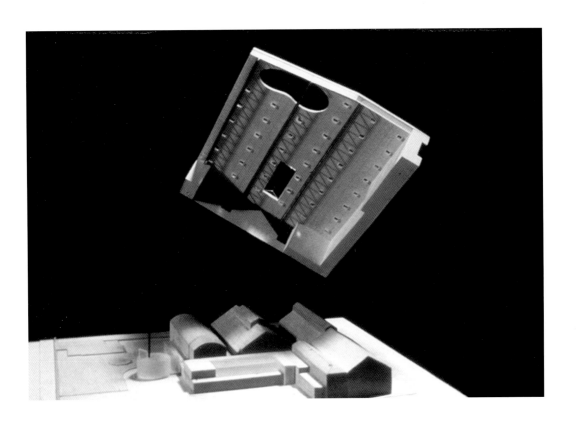

Works

Advertisements for Architecture
1976–1977

There is no way to perform architecture in a book. Words and drawings can only produce paper space, not the experience of real space. By definition, paper space is imaginary: it is an image.

Several of Tschumi's early theoretical texts were illustrated with *Advertisements for Architecture*, a series of postcard-sized juxtapositions of words and images. Each was a manifesto of sorts, confronting the dissociation between the immediacy of spatial experience and the analytical definition of theoretical concepts. The function of the *Advertisements*—reproduced again and again, as opposed to the single architectural piece—was to trigger desire for something beyond the page itself. When removed from their customary endorsement of commodity values, advertisements are the ultimate magazine form, even if used ironically. The logic presumes that since there are advertisements for architectural products, why not advertisements for the production (and reproduction) of architecture?

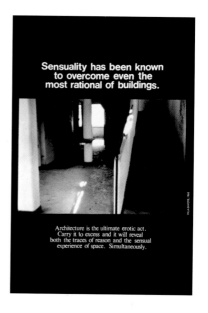

Sensuality has been known to overcome even the most rational of buildings.

Architecture is the ultimate erotic act.
Carry it to excess and it will reveal
both the traces of reason and the sensual
experience of space. Simultaneously.

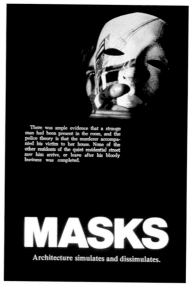

There was ample evidence that a strange man had been present in the room, and the police theory is that the murderer accompanied his victim to her house. None of the other residents of the quiet residential street saw him arrive, or leave after his bloody business was completed.

MASKS
Architecture simulates and dissimulates.

To really appreciate architecture, you may even need to commit a murder.

Architecture is defined by the actions it witnesses as much as by the enclosure of its walls. Murder in the Street differs from Murder in the Cathedral in the same way as love in the street differs from the Street of Love. Radically.

The most architectural thing about this building is the state of decay in which it is.

VILLA SAVOYE, 1965

Architecture only survives
where it negates the form that
society expects of it.
Where it negates itself by
transgressing the limits that
history has set for it.

If you want to follow architecture's first rule, break it.

Transgression.
An exquisitely perverse act
that never lasts.
And like a caress is
almost impossible to resist.

TRANSGRESSION

"The Garden of Forking Paths," by Jorge Luis Borges

"An ivory labyrinth!" I exclaimed. "A minimum labyrinth."
"A labyrinth of symbols," he corrected. "An invisible labyrinth
of time. To me, a barbarous Englishman, has been entrusted the
revelation of this diaphanous mystery. After more than a hundred years, the details are irretrievable; but it is not hard to
conjecture what happened. Ts'ui Pên must have said once: *I am
withdrawing to write a book*. And another time: *I am withdrawing to construct a labyrinth*. Every one imagined two works; to
no one did it occur that the book and the maze were one and
the same thing. The Pavilion of the Limpid Solitude stood in
the center of a garden that was perhaps intricate; that circum-
stance could have suggested to the heirs a physical labyrinth.
Ts'ui Pên died; no one in the vast territories that were his came
upon the labyrinth; the confusion of the novel suggested to me
that *it* was the maze. Two circumstances gave me the correct
solution of the problem. One: the curious legend that Ts'ui Pên
had planned to create a labyrinth which would be strictly infinite.
The other: a fragment of a letter I discovered."

Behind every great city, there's a garden.

Look at it this way:

The game of architecture is an intricate
play with rules that you may break or accept.
These rules, like so many knots that cannot
be untied, have the erotic significance of
bondage: the more numerous and sophisticated
the restraints, the greater the pleasure.

ropes and rules

The most excessive passion
always involves a set of rules.
Why not enjoy them?

e ROT ic
(the 'rotten' place)

where glass meets mold

Screenplays
1978

The Screenplays *are investigations of concepts as well as techniques, proposing simple hypotheses and then testing them out. They explore the relation between events ("the program") and architectural spaces, on one hand, and transformational devices of a sequential nature, on the other.*

The use of film images in these works originated in Tschumi's interest in sequences and programmatic concerns. ("There is no architecture without action, no architecture without event, no architecture without program.") Rather than composing fictional events or sequences, it seemed more informative to act upon existing ones.

The cinema thus was an obvious source. At the same time, the rich formal and narrative inventions of the only genuine 20th-century art inevitably encouraged parallels with current architectural thought. Flashbacks, crosscutting, jumpcuts, dissolves and other editing devices provided a rich set of analogies to the time-and-space nature of architecture. Yet the concerns of the *Screenplays* were essentially architectural. They dealt with issues of material (generators of form: reality, abstraction, movement, events, and so forth), device (disjunction, distortion, repetition, and superimposition), and counterpoint (between movement and space, events and spaces, for example). The *Screenplays* aimed at developing a contemporary set of architectural tools.

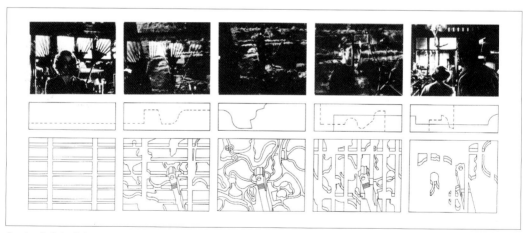

Psycho. Fade-in, fade-out

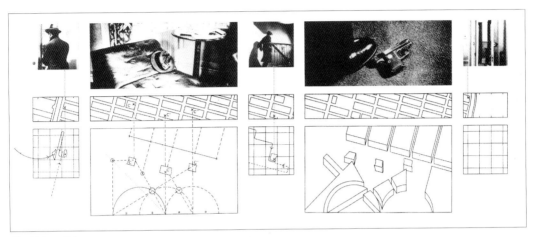

The Maltese Falcon

Frankenstein. Materialization

The Manhattan Transcripts
1976–1981

Architecture is not simply about space and form, but also about event, action, and what happens in space.

The Manhattan Transcripts differ from most architectural drawings insofar as they are neither real projects nor mere fantasies. Developed in the late 1970s, they proposed to transcribe an architectural interpretation of reality. To this aim, they employed a particular structure involving photographs that either directed or "witnessed" events (some would call them "functions," others "programs"). At the same time, plans, sections, and diagrams outlined spaces and indicated the movements of the different protagonists intruding into the architectural "stage set." The *Transcripts'* explicit purpose was to transcribe things normally removed from conventional architectural representation, namely the complex relationship between spaces and their use, between the set and the script, between "type" and "program," between objects and events. Their implicit purpose had to do with the 20th-century city.

The dominant theme of the *Transcripts* is a set of disjunctions among use, form, and social values; the non-coincidence between meaning and being, movement and space, man and object was the starting condition of the work. Yet the inevitable confrontation of these terms produced effects of far-ranging consequence. The Transcripts tried to offer a different reading of architecture in which space, movement and events were independent, yet stood in a new relation to one another, so that the conventional components of architecture were broken down and rebuilt along different axes.

While the programs used for *The Manhattan Transcripts* are of the most extreme nature, they also parallel the most common formula plot: the archetype of murder. Other phantasms were occasionally used to underline the fact that perhaps all architecture, rather than being about functional standards, is about love and death. By going beyond the conventional definition of use and program, the *Transcripts* used their tentative format to explore unlikely confrontations.

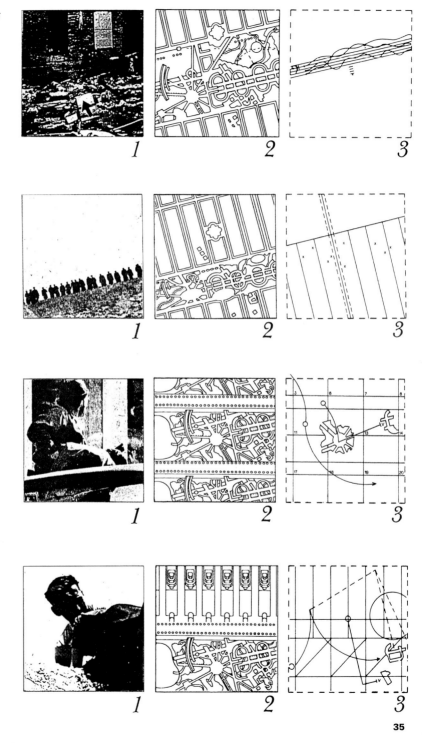

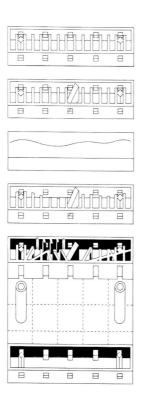

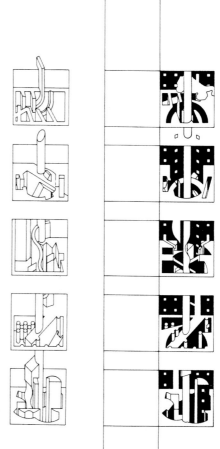

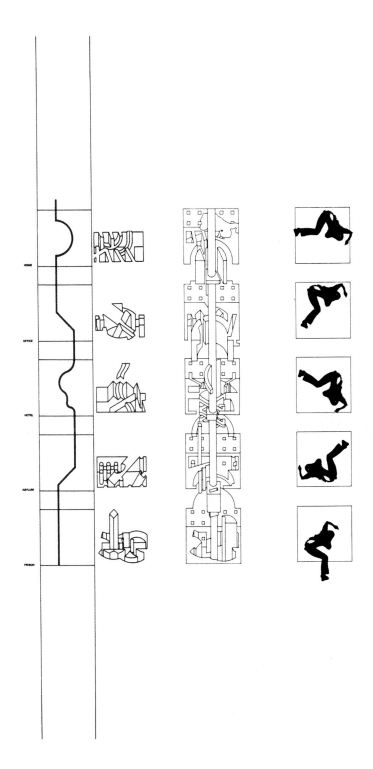

HOME

OFFICE

HOTEL

ASYLUM

PRISON

Joyce's Garden
1976–1977

The literary text, *Finnegans Wake*, was used as the program for a project involving a dozen contributions by different students on a "real" site, London's Covent Garden. The intersections of an ordinance survey grid became the locations of each architectural intervention, thereby accomodating a heterogeneous selection of buildings through the regular spacing of points. Moreover, the point grid functioned as a mediator between two mutually exclusive systems of words and stone, between the literary program and the architectural text. Joyce's Garden in no way attempted to reconcile the disparities resulting from the superimposition of one text on another; it avoided synthesis, instead encouraging the opposed and often conflicting logics of the different systems. Indeed, the abstraction of the grid as an organizing device suggested the disjunction between an architectural signifier and its programmatic signified, between space and the use that is made of it. The point grid became the tool of an approach that argued, against functionalist doctrines, that there is no cause-and-effect relationship between the two terms of program and architecture.

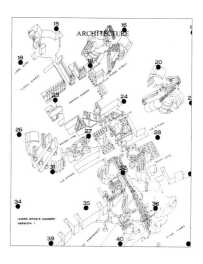

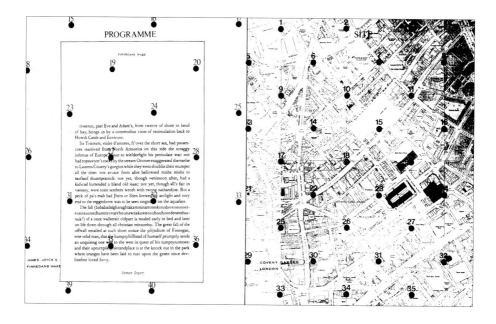

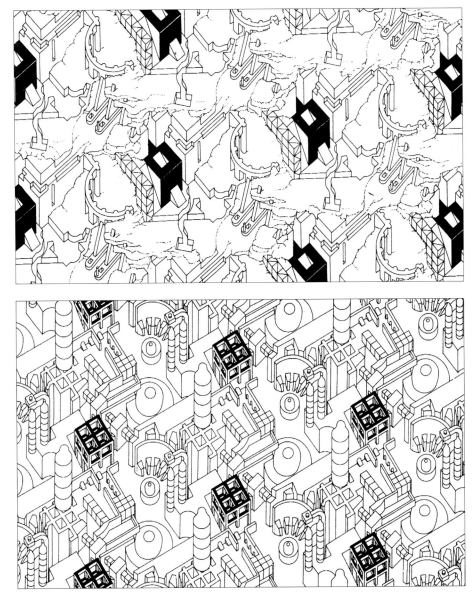

Parc de La Villette
Paris, France, 1982–1997

The competition for the Parc de la Villette was organized by the French Government in 1982. Its objectives were both to mark the vision of an era and to act upon the future economic and cultural development of a key area in Paris. As with other "Grands Projets" commissioned by President François Mitterand, such as the Opéra at Bastille, the Louvre Pyramid and the Arch at Tête-Defense, the Parc de la Villette was the center of numerous polemics, first at the time of the competition, when landscape designers protested the inclusion of architects, then during changes of government and budgetary crises.

The park is located on one of the last remaining large sites in Paris, a 125-acre expanse previously occupied by the central slaughterhouses and situated in the northeast corner of the city, between the Metro stations Porte de Pantin and Porte de la Villette. Over one kilometer long in one direction and seven hundred meters in the other, La Villette appears as a multiple programmatic field, containing, in addition to the park, the large Museum of Science and Industry, a City of Music, a Grande Halle for exhibitions, and a rock concert hall.

Despite its name, the park as designated in the competition was not to be a simple landscape replica. On the contrary, the brief for this "Urban Park for the 21st Century" developed a complex program of cultural and entertainment facilities, encompassing open-air theaters, restaurants and cafés, art galleries, music and video workshops, playgrounds and computer displays, as well as the obligatory gardens where cultural invention, rather than natural recreation, was encouraged. The object of the competition was to select a chief architect who would oversee the master plan and build the "structuring elements" of the park. Artists, landscape designers, and other architects were to contribute a variety of gardens or buildings.

The park scheme was selected over 471 other entries in a two-stage competition and built over a period of almost fifteen years. Its basis is the superimposition of three independent systems of Points, Lines and Surfaces:

1 Points
The folies are placed according to a point-grid coordinate system at 120-meter intervals throughout the park. The form of each is a basic 10 x 10 x 10 meter cube, or three-story construction of neutral space, that can be transformed and elaborated according to specific programmatic needs. Taken as a whole, the folies provide a common denominator for all of the events generated by the park program.

The repetition of folies is aimed at developing a clear symbol for the park, a recognizable identity as strong as the British public telephone booth or the Paris Metro gates. Their grid provides a comprehensive image or shape for an otherwise ill-defined terrain. Similarly, the regularity of routes and positions makes orientation simple for those unfamiliar with the area. An advantage of the point-grid system is that it provides for the minimum adequate equipment of the urban park relative to the number of its visitors.

2 Lines
The folie grid is related to a larger coordinate structure, an orthogonal system of high-density pedestrian movement that marks the site with a cross. The North-South Passage or Coordinate links the two Paris gates and subway stations of Porte de la Villette and Porte de Pantin; the East-West Coordinate joins Paris to its western suburbs. A five-meter-wide, open, waved covered structure runs the length of both Coordinates. Organized along the Coordinates so as to facilitate and encourage access are folies designated for the most frequented locations and activities, including the City of Music, cafés and restaurants, children's playgrounds, the first aid center, and music performances.

The Line system also includes the Path of Thematic Gardens, a seemingly random curvilinear route that links various parts of the park in a carefully-planned circuit. The Path of Thematic Gardens intersects the Coordinate axes at various places, providing unexpected encounters with unusual aspects of domesticated or "programmed" nature.

3 Surfaces
The park surfaces receive all activities requiring large expanses of horizontal space for play, sports and exercise, mass entertainment, markets, and so forth. During summer nights, for example, the central green becomes an open-air film theater for 3,000 viewers. So-called leftover surfaces, where all aspects of the program have been fulfilled, are composed of compacted earth and gravel, a park material familiar to Parisians.

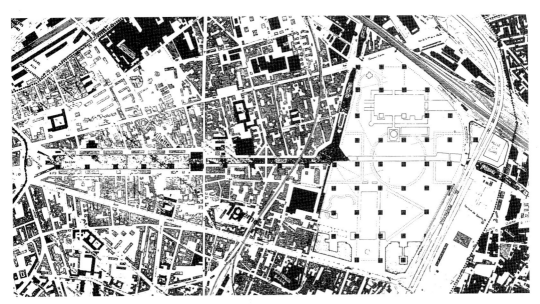

Site plan

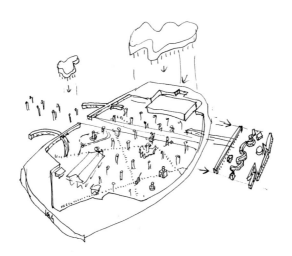

Our starting point is ideas or concepts, and the ways in which concepts relate to other disciplines and to different modes of thought. Architecture is not knowledge of form, but rather a form of knowledge. In other words, whenever we start to do something as architects we need to ask ourselves what architecture is. Architecture is not a pre-given thing. We architects always think that we define spaces by using walls, but the term "to define" also means to provide a definition or meaning. As architects, we need to constantly define and redefine what architecture is.

Exploding *folie*

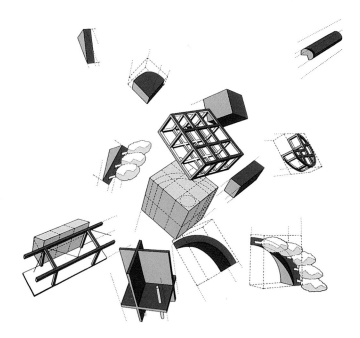

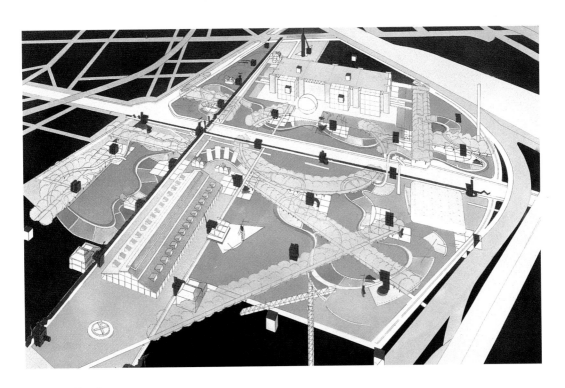

Superimposition: lines,
points, surfaces

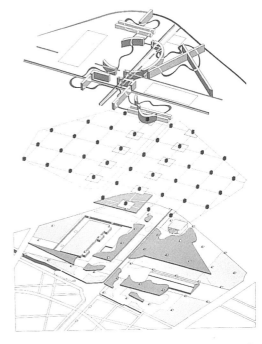

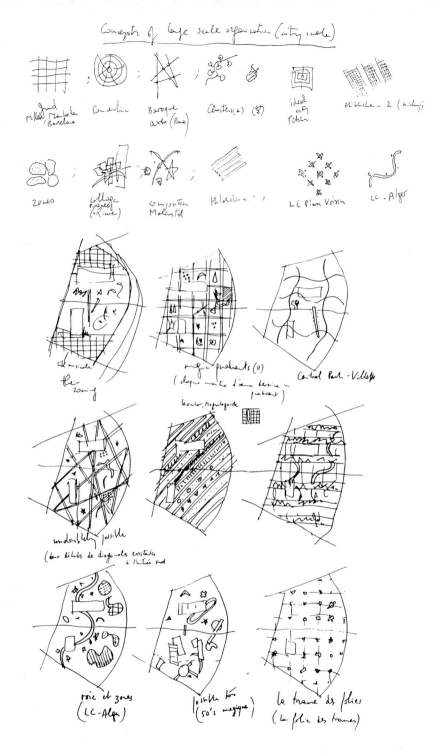

Concepts of large scale organisation (city scale)

Folie P6: prototype *folie*

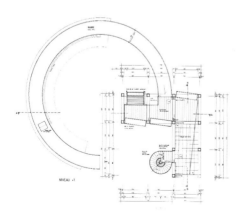

Folie P6: plan

Our project starts from the following thesis: there are building-generators of events. As much through their programs as through their spatial potential, they accelerate a cultural or social transformation that is already in progress.

Folie R7: jazz club, stage, bar

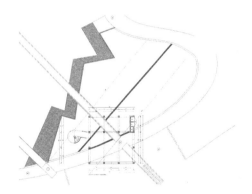

Folie R7: first floor

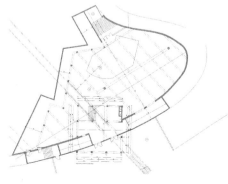

Folie R7: ground level

North-south gallery

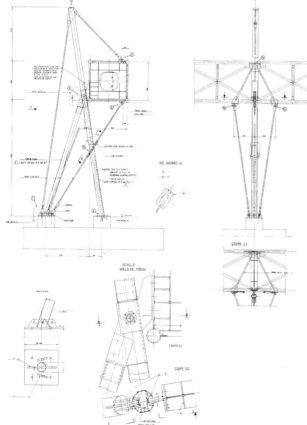

Construction detail: galleries

Architecture   Architecture
as form   as event
                VS.
a static definition   a dynamic definition
of architecture   of architecture

New National Theatre and Opera House
Tokyo, Japan, 1986

In this project for a national music performance facility, the traditional rules of composition and harmony were replaced by a mode of organization based not on "form follows function," "form follows form" or even "form follows fiction," but rather on breaking apart the conventional components of the theater and opera house in order to develop a new "tonality" or "sound."

The functional constraints of the building were extrapolated into a score of programmatic strips, each containing the main activities and related spaces in the following sequence:

1. A glass avenue that provides direct access from the subway, parking lot and buses. Its mezzanines or theater lobbies offer a vertical spectacle, while its ground floor gathers together crowds that employ different public services (box office, shops, bars, press office, reception areas, information, security and exhibition spaces). A restaurant is located between the glass avenue and the garden of the opera.

2. Vertical foyers that overlook the glass avenue and encompass coatrooms, box offices, bars or buffets, and suspended gardens. The border between the glass avenue and the vertical foyers is articulated by lighting for the avenue in the form of handrails, stairs, and so forth.

3. Auditoria acting as an acoustical strip, accommodating each audience in a minimum volume (thereby improving acoustical quality) with maximum visual access. This strip also accommodates VIP rooms, lavatories, and other services and allows for small, localized future programs at either end.

4. The strip coinciding with the proscenium, acting as a central artery servicing the whole complex.

5. The stages providing maximum flexibility and technical potential.

6. The strip containing the backstage area, assembly hall, rehearsal spaces and scenery workshops. Wherever possible, rehearsal and workshop spaces are provided with daylight.

7. The final strip serving artists and staff, containing dressing rooms and related spaces (which are organized along the balconies of a four-story artists' concourse, thereby avoiding the repetitiveness of corridors), as well as administrative offices that benefit from direct views of the opera garden.

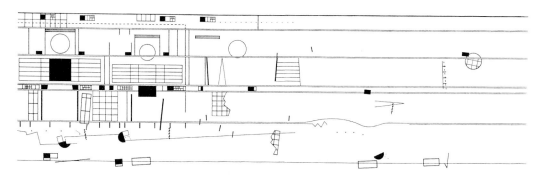

Linearity, juxtaposition, disintegration

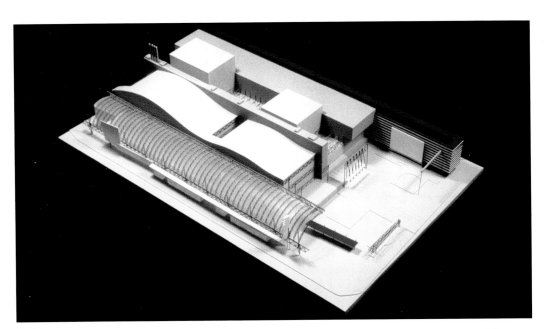

Model

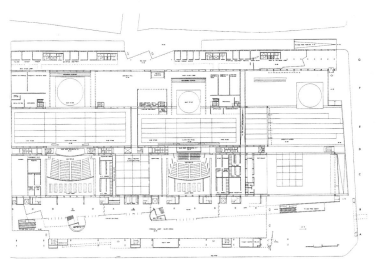

Plan at ground level

Center for Art and Media (ZKM)
Karlsruhe, Germany, 1989

The competition for the ZKM introduced a prototypical program for the late 20th century, the media and technology center, reflecting the new immanence of digital and electronic imagery in daily life. This project responded to the competition brief with a proposal composed of four parts, including a public passageway, a core, two specialized compartment spaces and an electronic "casing" or exterior.

1. The *urban line of exchange* is a linear public passage proposed as an alternative to the concentric Baroque structure of the historical Karlsruhe. It offers a new urban system based on communication and interchange placed at the historical edge of the city, luring the old limit into a new typology.

2. Located at the center of the building is a linear *core*, a public space with maximum visibility and excitement. The core and its balconies give access onto all parts of the facility. The ground floor contains the major performance, exhibition and seminar spaces; giant video screens, suspended *passerelles* and stairs, a glass elevator and two rooms appearing to float in midair activate an extensive and colorful foyer for the general public. This linear core allows for public "mediatization" of specialized research.

3. The two *compartments* located on each side of the linear core contain all specialized functions. The compartment on the north side contains most of the large spaces, such as the media theater, the contemporary art museum and the large elliptical studio. The south compartment contains smaller functions such as laboratories, offices and artists' studios, as well as the media gallery. On both sides, the more public spaces are located on the lower floors, the more specialized spaces on the upper floors.

The functional and construction systems of the two compartments are intentionally simple: repetitive cells on a regular concrete structure. The simplicity and sobriety of the building suggest that the emphasis of ZKM is placed on developing new media—on the construction of technology rather than the technology of construction.

4. The building is enclosed on the south side by an ever-changing, photo-electronic, computer-animated double-glazed skin or *casing* which reacts to variations in external light and sound. On the north side, the skin appears to emerge from a perforated stainless steel enclosure that connects with a copper-clad ellipse containing the multipurpose studio.

The digitized facade of the casing serves both as enclosure and as spectacle. Its perpetual change reminds us that if architecture once generated an image of stability, today it may also reveal the transience of unstable ones.

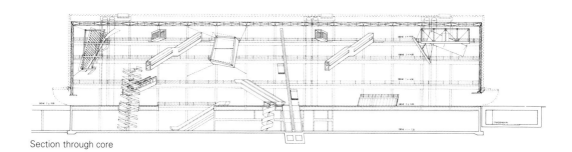

Section through core

Linear core

Urban line of exchange

National Library of France
Paris, France, 1989

This competition entry for France's National Library proposed a new type of library combining the pursuit of modernity with the pursuit of knowledge, the athlete with the scholar. The program was about circuits and movement—movement for scholars, books, and visitors—so the whole architectural scheme was developed around a constant dynamic. Opening simultaneously onto the Seine River, Paris, Europe and the rest of the world through the internal circuits of library culture, the building was also to act as an urban generator for a new part of the city. Inside, there were multi-media circuits for the public and circuits for the storage and retrieval of books. On the top part was an exhibition circuit and, outside, a running track, designed with the assumption that the athlete of the 21st century would be an intellectual and that the intellectual of the 21st century would be an athlete. Needless to say, the project lost the competition.

The fact that the library was not to be located in the historical center of Paris was considered a positive factor, encouraging a break away from earlier static concepts of libraries. The library was seen as an "event" rather than as a frozen monument. Locating a running track over the library embodied the building's complex role in developing an urban strategy that was expressed in the open circuit.

Within the new library, five interrelated sets of circuits can be identified: visitors' and administrators' circuits, book circuits, electronic circuits and mechanical circuits. While each has its own logic and set of rules, the circuits constantly interact at strategic locations.

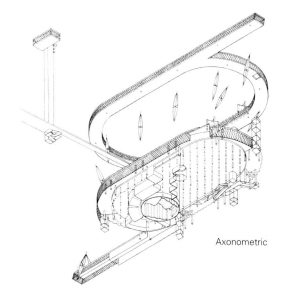

Axonometric

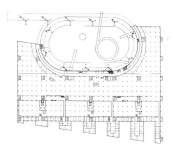

Fourth level plan (+25.20 m)

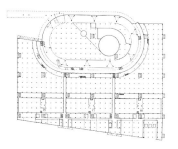

Mezzanine level plan (+6.50 m)

Exhibition circuit

Running track

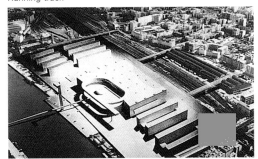

Site model photomontage

K-Polis Department Store
Zurich, Switzerland, 1995

The need for seduction through a language of display links department stores and museums. Within them, each exhibited product becomes an object of desire, and walking is the preferred means to apprehend such desirable objects. A slow dance begins between two bodies—the dynamic body of the visitor or consumer and the static body of the object of consumption.

The competition project for a new department store situated on the outskirts of Zurich attempts to express this dance. A ramp ascends in a random manner and intersects with all parts of the building. Like a long vector of movement, the ramp activates the building, defining intensity and areas of use. It is the "main street" of the Polis, open at late hours, as well as the route of the New. All new products are displayed along the ramp. Major night activities are located along the ramp and at the top of the new building. Roll-down gates and sliding glass partitions can separate the night section from the day section. The ramp is visible from inside through the large interior court, as well as from outside, where it pierces through the glass skin and through the advertising screen of the building.

The ramp occasionally intersects the envelope of the building and appears as a volume on the exterior. The envelope is made out of changing electronic signage integrated into layers of printed glass.

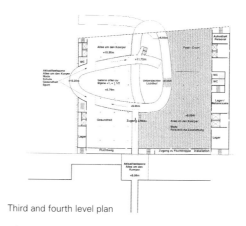

Third and fourth level plan

Roof level plan

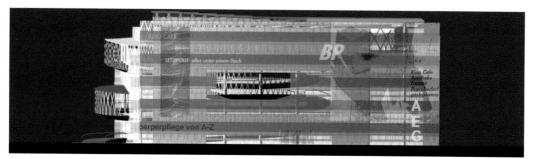

West elevation

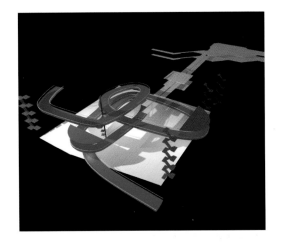

A random path

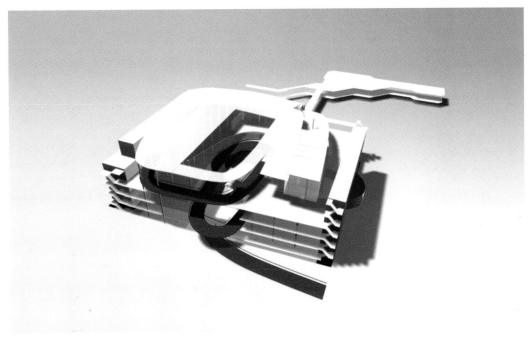

Model view

Kansai International Airport
Kansai, Japan, 1988

Airports no longer serve isolated functions. They are not unitary buildings, but now extend and redefine the metropolis. This project aimed to turn the proposed Kansai International Airport into a new type of metropolis, enlarging the airport into an event or spectacle–a city of interchange and exchange, business, commerce and culture. This 24-hour-a-day continuous invention was designed to act as a counterpoint to the city of Osaka, serving not only world travelers but also as a new urban segment for culture and recreation, with superstores and great hotels.

The airport is divided into two distinct parts, the linear city and the deck. The linear city consists of three lines: the double strip, the wave and the slab. The double strip contains all airport transfer functions in the terminal wings. The wave and the slab, key features of the project, are located between the two layers of the double strip. (Their dimensions are approximately eight meters for the slab and twelve meters for the wave.) The slab contains two hotels with a total of 1000 rooms as well as hour-rentable office space. The wave contains a mile-long entertainment, cultural and sports center, with cinemas, exhibition spaces, swimming pools, golf courses and shooting galleries, among other facilities.

The narrowness of the two bands not only reinforces the linearity of the new city, but forces an unprecedented density of events. The deck extends all the activities, from trade and commerce to art and culture, which take place in the linear city. With a non-directional structure that encompasses check-in counters, immigration offices and related services while allowing for extended tracts of space, it appears like an endless, four-story functional landscape.

The bands of the wave, slab, double strip and deck challenge traditional architecture by introducing spectacular parallel disjunctions. The interstices between the bands become as architecturally important as the bands themselves. Perceived by the visitor as stunning visual rifts, the linear negative spaces of these interstices question architectural composition by proposing unclassifiable spaces. Similarly, the distortion of the wave and its obliquely vertical axis question gravity: The datum plane ceases to be the ground and becomes a conceptual or technological parameter.

Section

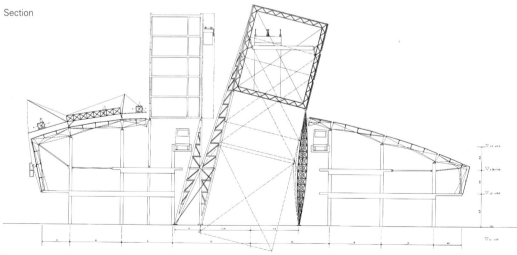

Linear city

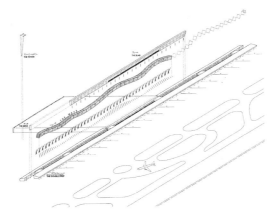

Double strip, wave, and slab

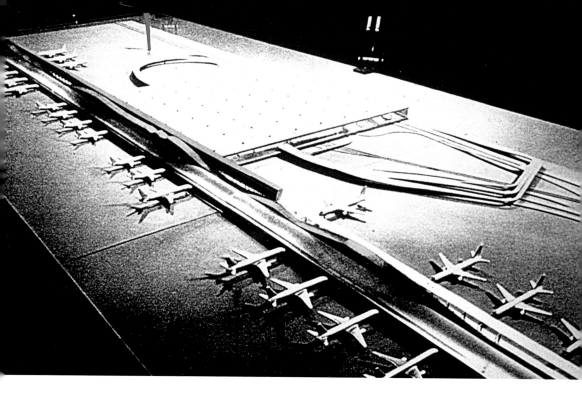

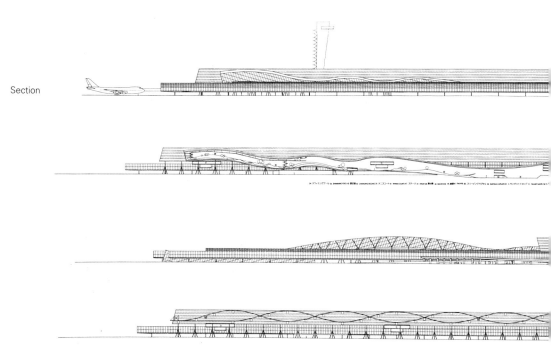

Section

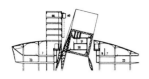

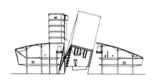

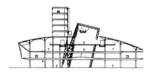

Sections through the wave

Interface Flon Railway and Bus Station
Lausanne, Switzerland, 1988–2001

Located in the heart of the Flon Valley at the Place de l'Europe, this station provides the beginning of an infrastructure network of transportation systems that will link Lausanne's center to its suburban peripheries. Four different lines of commuter services converge on the group of rectilinear steel-framed structures, sheathed in red-printed glass. The first phase, inaugurated and put in service in spring 2001, consists of the regional train and bus stations, elevators, a glass-enclosed bridge and a new traffic circle. The second phase will include a subway station, escalators with a glass envelope and an oblique plaza.

Part of a master plan won in competition in 1988, the project develops from the distinctive hilly topography of Lausanne, where streets appear as if suspended, buildings seem either buried in the ground or like vertical passageways, and bridges serve as multi-story crossings. The Interface is one of four "inhabited bridges" proposed in the master plan. Its ramps, escalators and elevators connect the lower levels of the valley, which currently are filled with industrial warehouses, to the upper levels of the historical city.

The different parts of the station are conceived as movement vectors in a dynamic circulation system. The station consists of 85,000 square meters of aboveground construction, with 3,500 square meters on the underground level. It is architecture as pure infrastructure.

East, west elevation

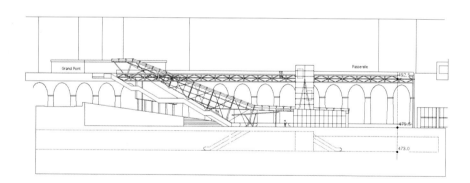

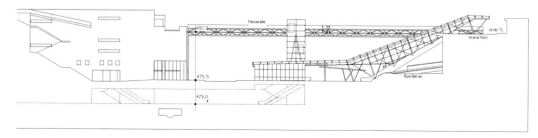

Street above, platform below

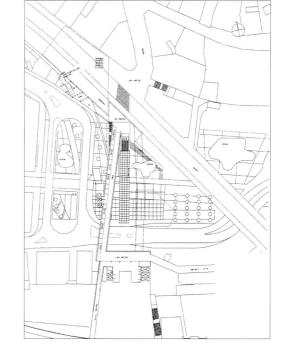

+472.50 m plan

Metropont

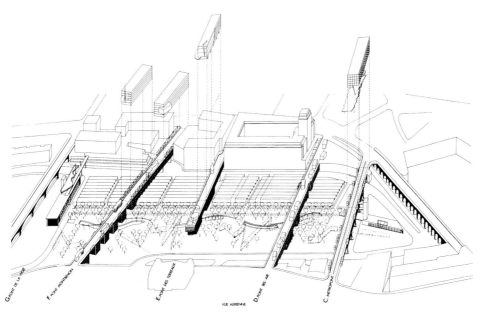

GPONT DE LA FEE   F PONT MONTEBRON   E PONT DES TERREAUX   VUE AERIENNE   D PONT BEL AIR   C METROPONT

The idea that architecture could be about vectors of movement became interesting in this project in Lausanne, a small Swiss city that spreads out over the hills by the lake. The project was literally about infrastructure in the form of bridge connections between the two parts of the valley. The heterogeneity is evident in the incredible mix of different realities at different spatial levels. The materiality of the glass is very important. When we start a project, not only do we start with a concept; we start with a material.

17th Street Loft
New York, New York, 1987

Located in the Chelsea district of Manhattan, this 4,800-square-foot loft enjoys fourteen windows facing south. To keep the space as unencumbered as possible and to generate large unprogrammed spaces, all rooms needing enclosure were arranged in a long rectangular box inserted longitudinally into the existing envelope of the loft. This strategy resulted in three parallel spatial layers as well as in secondary layers, all oriented in the same direction. Full-height metal bookshelves were then placed in the perpendicular direction as a mode of spatial notation. First used for work as well as for residential purposes, the loft is now a private residential space.

View looking west

View looking east

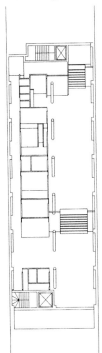

Rear corridor

The Hague Villa
The Hague, The Netherlands, 1992

Designing a small house in The Hague presented an opportunity to raise questions about the home and about assumptions of an impenetrable private domain. It also became a challenge to explore certain conditions of 21st-century living spaces. Could the house also be the place of the "event," ever-changing in the dematerialization of its electronic contents?

The glass enclosure of the living and work spaces, which measures 12 by 4 by 7 meters, is both transparent and translucent, due to the use of printed glass. It leans away from the rest of the house, revealing an in-between or interstitial connection. The heaviest part of the house, a concrete frame containing the bedrooms, is suspended over the remaining portion of domestic space, where the kitchen and storage are located. The bathroom crankshaft locks the other elements in place.

Conceived as a series of strips placed in between a canal, a major traffic road, housing and a park, the house extends these urban events while providing a momentary pause in the digital transfer of information. The borders of the living room and workspace, devoid of ornamental camouflage, expand beyond the property lines just as they are undermined by the electronic devices of everyday use (TV, fax, and so forth) that they contain.

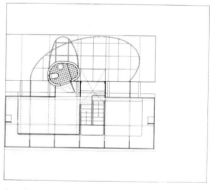

Level two

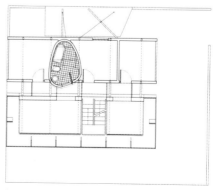

Level one

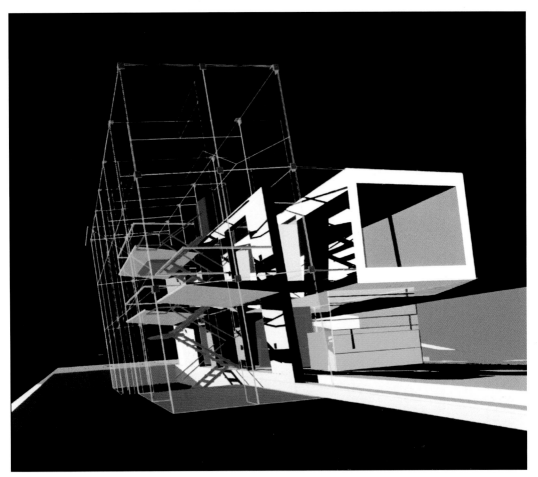

Domesti-city

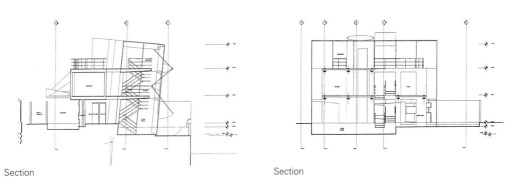

Section   Section

Glass Video Gallery
Groningen, The Netherlands, 1990

Commissioned by the city of Groningen as a temporary structure for a music and video festival, this video gallery is now a permanent work owned by the Groningen Museum. Designed on a small budget, it is a simple rectangular building made out of one material, glass. It responds to a contemporary architectural condition in which the appearance of permanence is increasingly challenged by the immaterial representation of abstract systems in the form of television and electronic images. The invitation to design a special environment for viewing pop-music videos, however, also offered opportunities to challenge preconceived ideas about spectatorship and privacy. Was the video gallery to be a static and enclosed black box, like the architectural type created for cinema; an extended living room with exterior advertising billboards and neon light; or a new "type" that brought what was previously a living room, bar or lounge event out into the street?

The video gallery is the first work by the architect to deal with the concept of the envelope. It is about the movement of the body as it travels through the exhibition space and about the enclosure, which is made entirely out of glass held by clips, including its vertical supports and horizontal beams. The resulting structure gives priority to the image. The monitors inside provide unstable facades, while the glass reflections create mirages, suggesting limitless space. At night, the space becomes an ensemble of mirrors and reflections, questioning what the real and the virtual are, and whether the envelope is an actual structure or an illusioned spectacle.

The glass video gallery proposes parallels to urban space, inasmuch as both contain video objects, or tapes, that are on display as well as objects for displaying them. These parallels extend to both the long monitor walls viewed through television dealership storefronts on the street and the sights visible in the sex-video galleries of urban red-light districts.

Entrance

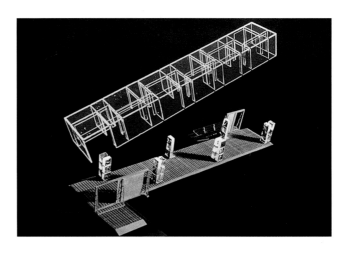

Axonometric

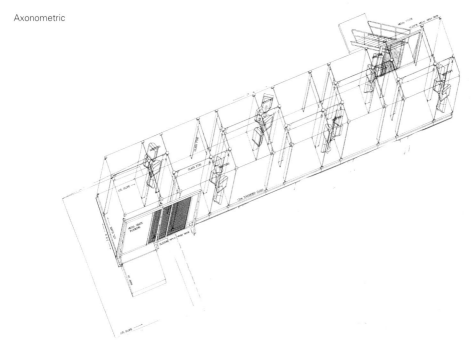

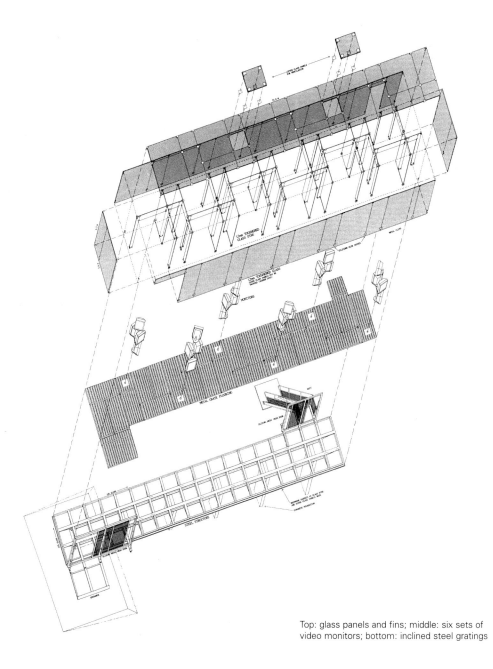

Top: glass panels and fins; middle: six sets of
video monitors; bottom: inclined steel gratings

Video Glass Gallery =
" undecidable "
envelopes

Endless reflections at night

Urban Glass House of the 21st Century

New York, New York, 1999

This house was commissioned by *Time* Magazine as a prototype for a dwelling of the future. It is an urban structure that responds to a contemporary desire for infinite space in the dense metropolis, reacting against the recurrent dream of Suburbia. Rather than abandoning the city and recreating an artificial urban experience outside of it, the house addresses the city by existing simultaneously inside and above it.

Precedents for the house are visible in Lower Manhattan, where penthouses have been constructed on top of warehouses and manufacturing buildings converted for residential use. The proposal suggests that similar penthouses could be built on high-rise buildings, brownstones and mega-blocks, where they would act as illuminated beacons, transparently celebrating domesticity and everyday life. Visible from below as well as from surrounding homes, they would "publicize privacy," offering a counterpoint to the Internet, which privatizes public life. The glass penthouses would also provide brilliant observation points on the on-going spectacle of the city down below.

The architecture of the Glass House plays on an opposition between an industrial-looking rectangular envelope and the lush curvature of its inner volumes. The glass-and-steel details of the exterior contrast with the soft curtains, polished marble, curved translucent glass and exotic-wood veneers of the interior.

Services and circulation are contained in an undulating "sandwich" wall that also assists in defining the living spaces. The wall expands and folds back, enclosing private spaces and opening to allow rooms and corridors to flow into one another. It provides the "subconscious" of the house, adjusting to the user's desires. Separations permitting greater privacy can be made by sliding partitions and curtains out from the service wall.

Bathrooms are contained in a large "wet" wall, made out of a composite of glass and resin, which extends through the house. The surface of this wall alternates between transparency or translucency and opacity. Its other side is a digital wall that acts as a projection screen, or media installation, for pliable electronic images. This curved wall could convey blown-up enlargements of the most intimate moments of its occupants' everyday lives or, should they prefer more anonymity, messages from advertising slogans to movies to exhibitions of their video art collection.

The intermediate floor plate of the house is cantilevered from within the undulating double wall. Services such as water and electricity simply "plug into" the existing facilities of the underlying building.

Glass house in the sky

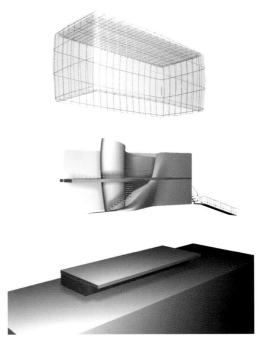

Night view

Le Fresnoy National Studio for the Contemporary Arts
Tourcoing, France, 1991–1997

Le Fresnoy is a center for multimedia art crossovers, such as a video artist who is also a musician or a musician who is a filmmaker or painter. The site is exceptional because it integrates the buildings of an old leisure complex from the 1920s that included cinema, ballroom dancing, skating, horseback riding and other activities. Although the existing structures could have been demolished to make way for new construction, they contained extraordinary spaces whose large dimensions exceeded what the limited project budget could supply. Because the artistic and pedagogical project was unique and absolutely innovative, the architectural project needed to be equally unprecedented. The aim was to develop a new model of a center through combinations of old and new, development and production, artistic practice and public exhibition.

The project suspends a large, ultra-technological roof, pierced by cloud-like glass openings and containing all necessary ductwork for heating, ventilation and air conditioning, over many of the existing '20s structures. The format of the project is of a succession of boxes inside a box. First, a new, resolutely contemporary facade encloses the ensemble of buildings in a rectangular box. The north side of the box is made out of corrugated steel, while the curtain wall facades of the southern sector give a transparent image to the entrance and main building facade. The other sides remain open, providing views of the old and new within and of the technical ductwork suspended under the new roof and over the old ones. Within the container-box are the boxes of the existing Fresnoy facilities, supplemented by newly-designed ones, all of them protected from inclement weather by the vast umbrella of the new roof.

The new facilities have been located in the existing volumes as technically autonomous boxes while maintaining the fluidity of the old spaces. The different areas include exhibition spaces in the old halls, sound studios and assorted production facilities, a library, a cinema, a restaurant and apartments for faculty and students. A zone of economic activity or commercial space is integrated into the project as a fourth hall in the south end of the existing vaulted hall. An underground parking lot is to be provided under the commercial spaces and the administrative offices.

The "in-between" space between the new steel and old tile roofs is the key element of the project. Large horizontal windows, cut into the steel in cloud shapes and covered with transparent sheets of polycarbonate, create an underside flooded with light and divided by a transversal corresponding to the project's north-south axis. The spaces between the two roofs contain places for installations and film projections located along a dramatic sequence of walkways. A landscaped terrace in front of the restaurant and bar profits from direct access from street-level through the grand staircase.

The new roof acts as the project's common denominator, a kind of sheltering and all-encompassing umbrella. In keeping with the Surrealist image of the meeting of the umbrella and the sewing machine on the dissecting table, the scheme of the project aims to accelerate chance events by combining diverse elements, juxtaposing the great roof, the school and research laboratory, and the old Fresnoy, a place of spectacle. The whole is precise and rational in its concept, and varied and poetic in the resulting spatial richness.

View from Rue du Fresnoy

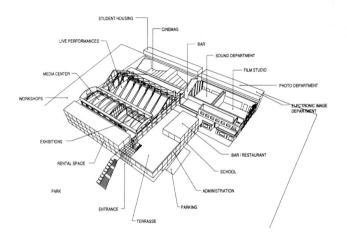

Program

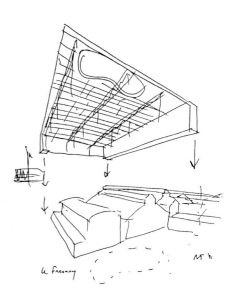

Existing conditions

View from west

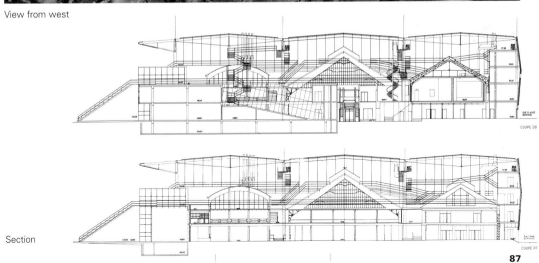

Section

The in-between

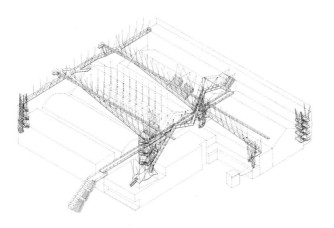

The in-between: catwalks

View towards main entry

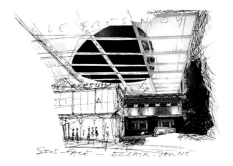

Grand stair

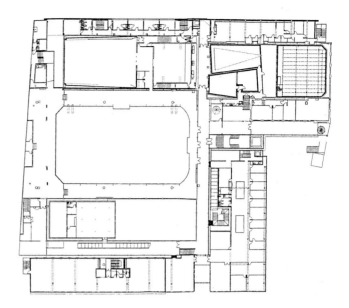

Ground level

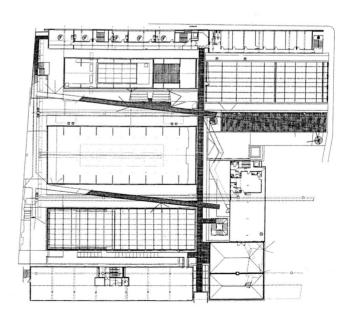

Level +7.43 m

TO ACHIEVE ARCHITECTURE WITHOUT RESORTING
TO DESIGN IS AN AMBITION OFTEN IN THE MINDS OF THOSE
WHO GO THROUGH THE UNBELIEVABLE EFFORT OF PUTTING
TOGETHER BUILDINGS.

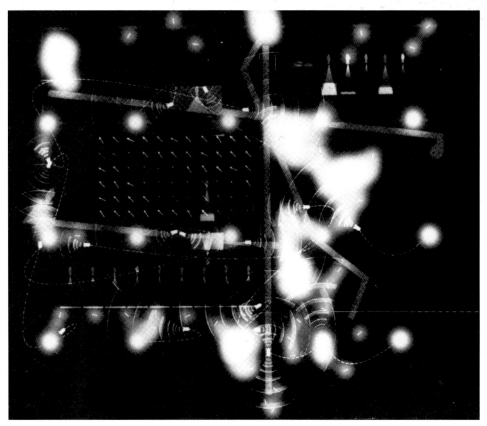

Simulated night view of in-between

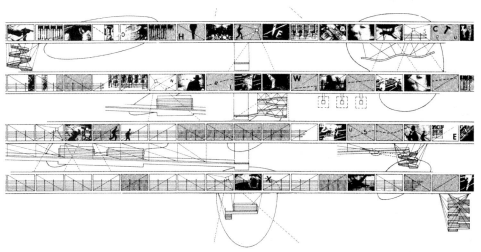

Cinematic trusses

Alfred Lerner Hall Student Center, Columbia University

New York, New York, 1994–1999*

The design of the new student center for Columbia University proved to be challenging because of the requirement that it fit within the university's historical master plan, a 19th-century neoclassical composition by the firm McKim Mead and White. The strategy adopted works within the regulating lines of the original plan, which mandated double wings, and places the major innovation in the "in-between" space inside them. The two traditional wings are connected by a radically new type of ramp, with the different features of the program organized along it. The ramps employ the most advanced level of glass-and-steel technology available.

The required functional rooms are situated inside the double rectangular volumes, while large public spaces such as the main lobby, auditorium and black box theater were developed between the two wings. The two wings used the brick and granite materials prevalent in the historical campus, while the space between them is as transparent as current technology allows. Glass ramps criss-cross the void, connecting the different levels and activities of the student center, while a huge glass wall, with panes attached through point-fixing, extends the length of the void, bringing the maximum amount of light into the building and allowing a striking view over the campus outside. The dramatic void-space or "hub" is animated and defined by the movement of students and visitors along the ramps. Three thousand mailboxes required for student mail provide a backdrop for this motion along the southern length of the ramps.

The ramps also respond to a topographical feature of the site, by which the street or "Broadway" level of the building is one half-story lower than the opposite "Campus" side. The eight-story Broadway wing includes the cinema and assembly hall, bookstore, game rooms, student clubs, a radio station and three floors of academic and administrative spaces. The cinema and assembly hall, which seats 400 people, is located so that, by folding its screen, it can act as a balcony to the 1100-seat auditorium below, bringing the auditorium capacity to 1500. The Campus wing contains restaurants and a café, conference and practice rooms, a travel agency and a student nightclub. The myriad activities that take place around the central void of the ramps are also visible from a series of lounges placed around its perimeter. The number and scope of those activities make the student center seem like a small city, at once traversed and animated by the dynamic circulation system of the ramps.

The project adopts a "normative" approach to the outside, responding to the McKim plan, while the inner void space deviates from the norm in inventive ways. Similarly, the building is quiet on the outside and filled with activity on the inside. Tschumi has said that he approached the brick-and-granite rules of the McKim master plan as an *objet trouvé*, a Duchamp-like found object to oppose to the innovative potential of the interstitial spaces between the wings. The result is a hybrid building in which the values of a singular style, esthetic or sensibility are contrasted with the clarity of an architectural strategy.

*With Gruzen Samton Associated Architects

The ramps

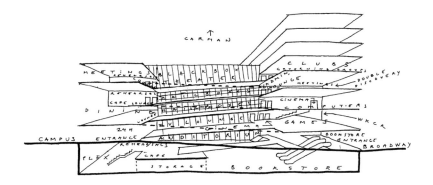

The hub

Evolution of the 19th-century master plan

View from Broadway

Reflective superimposition

Installation of the ramps

View of campus

The hub

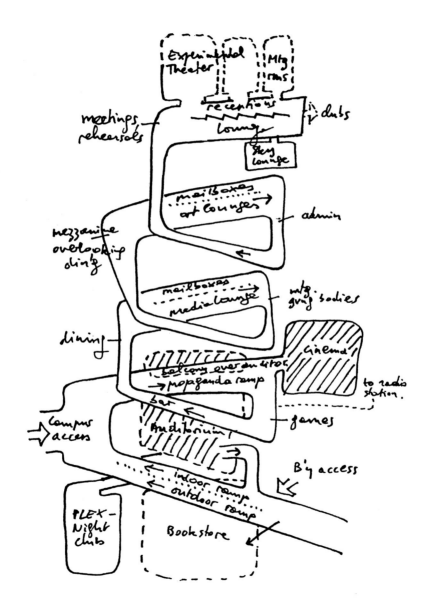

Ramp detail

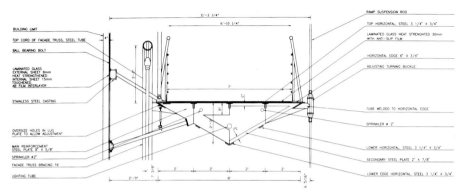

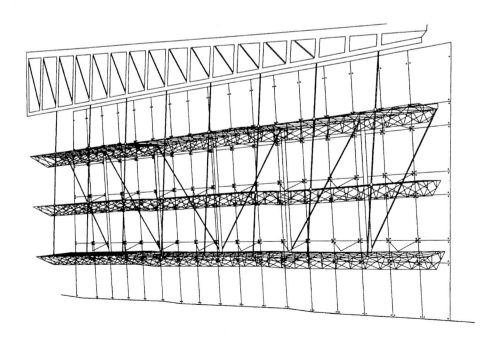

SECTION A-A — ARM CONNECTION TO RAMP

Ramp at night

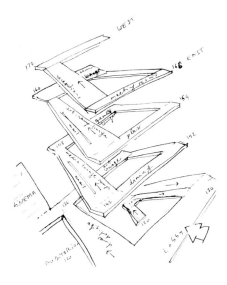

The hub: lounge overlooking auditorium

The hub

In many ways I prefer the images of Lerner with people because they show what the building is for. In other words, the building is always about movement in space. Architecture is not about creating a static envelope. One day, a dance company decided to use the building for a performance. People were sitting outside the building and looking into the spectacle on the ramps. They had understood the building.

Expansion of The Museum of Modern Art
New York, New York, 1997

In 1997 The Museum of Modern Art held a two-phase competition to expand and re-think its existing facilities, located on West 53rd Street in Manhattan. In the first phase, ten architects were invited to develop their thoughts in the form of drawing sketchbooks; in the second, three from among the initial ten were asked to elaborate these reflections into concrete proposals. Bernard Tschumi Architects was one of the three finalists, and developed a complex exploration of the urban and exhibition needs confronting the museum as it moved into the 21st century. The following are edited excerpts from the sketchbook-phase submission:

The site reproduces a characteristic situation of today's world, in which older metropolises are overbuilt, filled with architectural treasures or buildings of sufficient historical significance not to be demolished. A beloved garden in their midst further complicates the situation. Moreover, the massing of new construction on adjacent sites is mostly predetermined by the restrictive zoning regulations in this part of New York.

This situation requires a strategy that accounts for existing constraints in addition to new museum needs. This means that at no moment can the expansion be conceived of as a self-sufficient totality; each part will function fully only in conjunction with another, older or newer part. Moreover, the existing site conditions rule against starting from the outside, and in favor of starting from the inside, carving a series of interior spaces that would be somewhat like an outside, but inside.

A crucial dimension is the concept of carving spaces into a solid. The solid would be made out of the existing buildings and notional envelopes defined by zoning regulations. The carved spaces would trace an urban route with "streets" and "squares" or "plazas" linking the exhibition spaces and functions, describing one or multiple paths through the museum. The building would be somewhat like a city carved into a mass of solid matter, with careful filtering and distribution of light into the core.

The spatial organization of the new MoMA reflects our view that architectural considerations are never independent of urban circumstances, and the internal logic of a building must respond to its external conditions. In order to reflect its own "historicity," the new MoMA may have to introduce a new form of museum by reversing conventional a priori. We propose three reversals, which, together, constitute an operative concept rather than an arbitrary arrangement of forms:

First reversal: The museum is not conceived as a sculptural object, but as an interior city or route. Its exterior form must be derived from and expressive of its interior dimensions. Moreover, the route is not a linear sequence with a fixed beginning, middle, and end, but a multiple sequence that can be accessed or departed from at many points.

Second reversal: The new Museum of Modern Art is not a unitary totality, but a heterotopia. It combines three distinct types: a received type, the 25-foot-square column grid and double bay of the historical MoMA, for its departments; a borrowed type, the columnless factory type, for its temporary exhibitions; and a new type, our proposal for fixed spaces, variable spaces, and interspaces, for the permanent collection.

Third reversal: The third reversal is strategic rather than constructed. It is about architecture as strategy as much as about architecture as form. The constraints of the site, program, and zoning regulations are such that imposing a simple external model would be a losing proposition. A different strategy is required, akin to Judo, in which the forces of the opponent are used to one's advantage. The site conditions, historical and artistic heterogeneity of the museum, and the demands of new art are productive forces, requiring a reversal of architectural conventions.

Together, these three reversals introduce a new model for the urban museum in the 21st century.

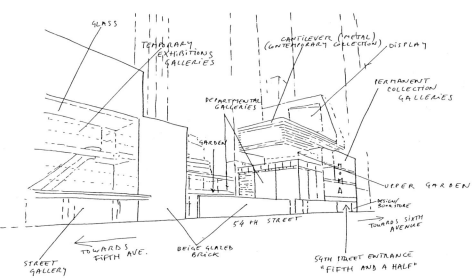

GLASS

TEMPORARY
EXHIBITIONS
GALLERIES

CANTILEVER (METAL)
(CONTEMPORARY COLLECTION) DISPLAY

PERMANENT
COLLECTION
GALLERIES

DEPARTMENTAL
GALLERIES

GARDEN

UPPER GARDEN

DESIGN/
BOOKSTORE

54 TH STREET

TOWARDS SIXTH
AVENUE

TOWARDS
FIFTH AVE.

BEIGE GLAZED
BRICK

54TH STREET ENTRANCE
"FIFTH AND A HALF"

STREET
GALLERY

Flows & voids

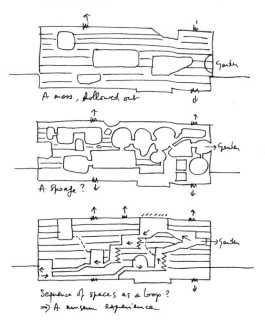

A mass, hollowed out

A sponge?

Sequence of spaces as a loop?
⇒ A museum experience

" a mode of spacing that gives its place to events "

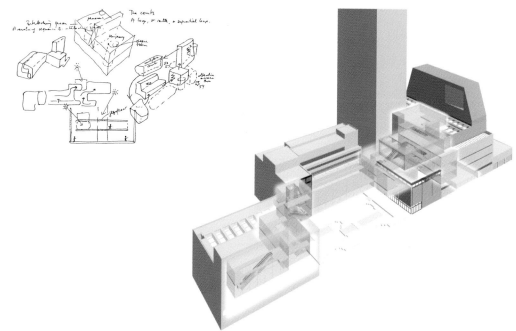

The courts: a sequence of art and social spaces

View from street

Museums are about time: the times of history and of motion through space. This project was about movement organized in such a way that it would generate public spaces. The concept of the project was that the different parts of the museum would present a series of vertical areas to be used as public spaces with a view onto the city. The main idea was that movement and spaces have an inherently public nature. In other words, architecture is something that offers a "place" to public events.

Tower court

Cantilevered gallery

School of Architecture
Marne-la-Vallée, France, 1994–
first phase completed 1999

This building for a new school of architecture, located 30 minutes by car outside of Paris, raises two questions. The first has to do with the direction that architectural education will take in the next decades. The second has to do with the attraction that a school situated on the periphery or margin of the social, economic and cultural density of an urban center can have.

The school takes as its "site" a triple revolution—informational, interdisciplinary and ideological—that is in the making today. A fundamental premise is that Marne-la-Vallée is at the same electronic distance from London, Berlin, Tokyo, New York, or Delhi. In the midst of this global architectural culture and information, the marginal or decentered location of the school appears as an advantage; removed from habits of thought related to the conservation of historical centers, the site, set amidst a new 20,000-student technological complex developed by the French government, provides a starting point for a model of a school for the age of the modern and mobility.

The design of the school begins from the thesis that there are "building-generators" of events. Such structures are often condensers of the city. Through their programs as much as through their spatial qualities, they accelerate or intensify a cultural and social transformation that is already in progress.

In this two-phase construction, all of the programmed activities are arranged around a large longitudinal space, measuring 25 by 100 meters, which is activated by the density of what surrounds it. The space is designed as a place for celebrations and balls, encounters and debates, projections and artists' installations, as well as for the most serious symposia and avant-garde exhibitions. The functional and programmatic parts of the school, including studios, computer labs, a mediathèque, faculty offices and administration and research areas, open onto this interior rectangle. Similarly, the activity in the studios is visible from the longitudinal hall, reinforcing the image of the school as a place of communication and discussion.

The circulation is also gathered together in this longitudinal hall. Staircases and steel walkways criss-cross the space, and the studios and other functional spaces all give onto corridors that ring the space in a multi-leveled suite of open passageways. This transforms the building into a large promenade, with several points of departure (the building has two entrances, one of which also leads to an underground parking lot) as well as multiple shortcuts through it. The first-phase, 100-seat amphitheater–a striking "object" posed within the space and covered in shimmering extruded metal—can be accessed by stairs and by walkways. The space below it offers a gallery for exhibitions adjoining the student bar, while the amphitheater roof is a multipurpose environment available for dances, gatherings or seminars.

The roof of the second-phase, 400-seat amphitheater acts as a public space for exhibitions and project reviews. By 2002, the building was still truncated, as various government agencies had not given the go-ahead for the second phase.

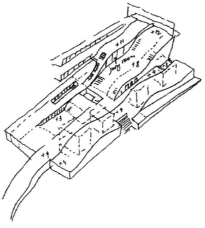

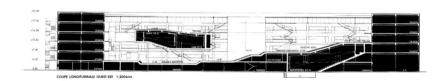

COUPE LONGITUDINALE OUEST-EST 1:200mm

Section through
central hall

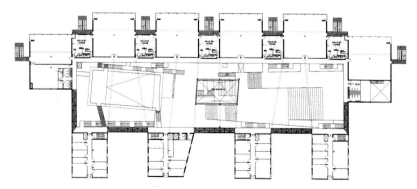

+10.5 m plan

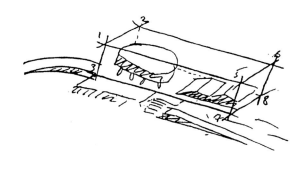

FIU School of Architecture
Miami, Florida, 1999–2003

Florida International University is located in the largest and fastest-growing metropolis in the southeastern United States, a city that combines glamour with commerce and is situated at the epicenter of a zone of influence that extends into the Caribbean and South America. This major new building for FIU's School of Architecture and College of Urban and Public Affairs therefore has the potential to become a hub of ideas between two major cultures. The project proposes that a new school of architecture has the ability to set a stage or scene for cultural development and to become identified with it, and that its new building must contribute to making that scene and that identity. The building must act as a "generator," activating spaces as well as defining them.

The young school of architecture at FIU has been described as a commuter school, in which students divide their time among an office where they earn a living, the school where they study, and the home where they often oversee family responsibilities. This situation, often considered an impediment, can be turned into an advantage: the design for the new facility reflects the argument that computer technology has freed designers from the fixity of the drafting table. Disks and files can be e-mailed instantly anywhere, so that the location of actual work becomes secondary. What is primary, however, is the social exchange—the discussion, debate, and clash of ideas among friends, colleagues and teachers—which can only happen at the school.

The thesis that buildings can encourage events and interaction informs the basic scheme, which can be described as two "sober" wings defining a space activated by the exuberance of three colorful "generators." The wings are made of white pre-cast concrete; the generators of, respectively, variegated yellow ceramic tiles and variegated red ceramic tiles (for the two individual buildings) and nature (Royal Palm trees).

In a concept that has similarities to the one employed at Marne-la-Vallée, requested programmed activities are arranged around a central courtyard measuring 60 by 90 feet that is activated by two generators located on either end. One contains a lecture hall; the other, an exhibition gallery and reading room. Studios, classrooms and faculty and administrative offices are situated in the two wings. Jury and review rooms in the studio wing overlook the courtyard, whose dimensions and disposition encourage encounter, discussion and celebration. Gathering together the school's circulation as well as its main social and cultural spaces, the central generators also shade the courtyard during the morning and late afternoon hours, responding to the hot local climate. Whatever the level of attendance on any given day, a constant movement of students is visible on the shaded steps, along the periphery, and on the unprogrammed space above the lecture hall, giving the court liveliness and dynamism.

Section through generators

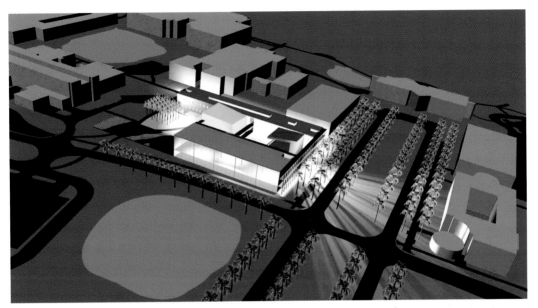

Campus view

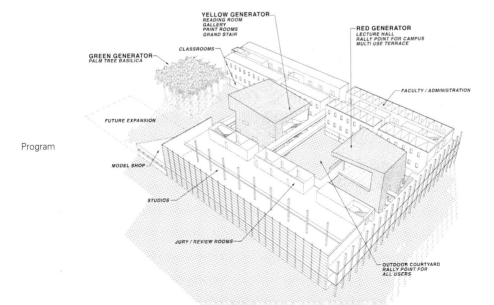

Program

GREEN GENERATOR
PALM TREE BASILICA

YELLOW GENERATOR
READING ROOM
GALLERY
PRINT ROOMS
GRAND STAIR

CLASSROOMS

RED GENERATOR
LECTURE HALL
RALLY POINT FOR CAMPUS
MULTI USE TERRACE

FACULTY / ADMINISTRATION

FUTURE EXPANSION

MODEL SHOP

STUDIOS

JURY / REVIEW ROOMS

OUTDOOR COURTYARD
RALLY POINT FOR
ALL USERS

119

In Miami, we worked on the notion of treating the parts of the building that have a public nature—the auditorium, gallery and library—as generators, like the points of intensity of the folies at Parc de la Villette. Two wings define the more conventional parts of the program, classrooms and architecture studios. These wings define in-between spaces activated by the two generators along with the group of palm trees that becomes the third generator. We also asked whether movement flows could affect the geometry of the buildings. Computer modeling through fluid mechanics software determined the geometry of the architecture. Architecture is never a form per se; it is always defined through event and movement.

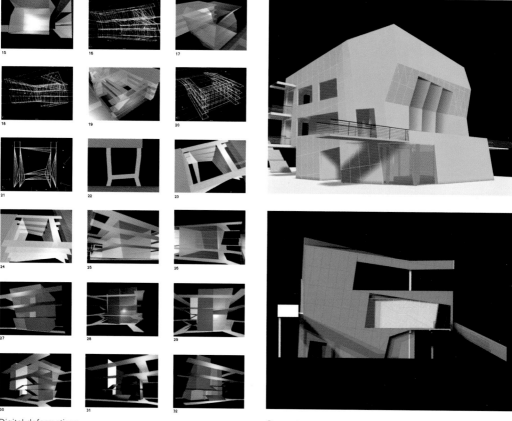

Digital deformations

Generators

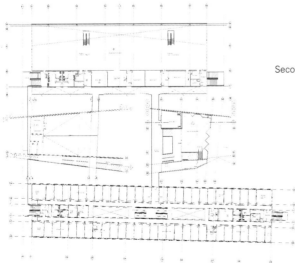

Second floor plan

Business Park
Chartres, France, 1991

This project for a 450-acre expansion of the city of Chartres through an office park, indoor leisure facilities, sports fields and a housing complex proposes a relationship between work and leisure that is based on intersection and superimposition rather than segregation. The site faces the city and its famed cathedral, and is located on agricultural land fronting a national highway.

A strong link to the city is established through the *longcours*, a vector leading to and from the center of Chartres and the cathedral. This vector gathers together the leisure facilities, a clubhouse, meeting halls, shops and so forth within the enveloping form of curved halls. Each construction is partially suspended and provides a shelter for a variety of public events. The longcours can also accommodate facilities such as an open-air cinema, a swimming pool and tennis courts. It extends west over the highway, acting as a bridge to Chartres, and east towards the countryside.

A second vector was proposed extending parallel to the highway, with grids to accommodate numerous plots of land defined by lines of trees. The grids permit light factories and office buildings to be constructed within the defined plots of land. Office spaces are also located in ship-like buildings scattered within the acreage. Neon signage is proposed throughout.

Long parallel rows of trees planted perpendicular to the gridded office vector articulate the landscape. Sports facilities, playgrounds and entertainment centers are located within the linear plantings.

The scheme is conceived according to a gaming strategy that permits the complex programmatic mechanisms of the business park to coincide with the conceptual clarity of its built image.

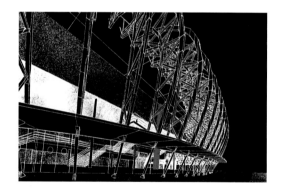
Meeting hall

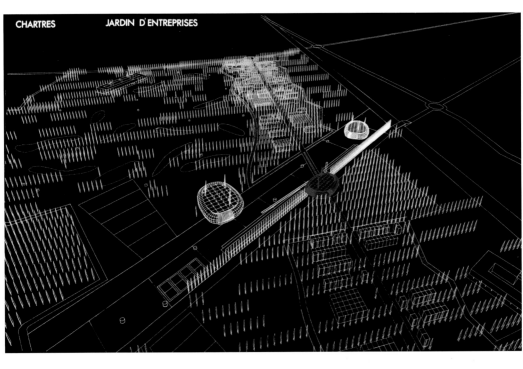

CHARTRES   JARDIN D'ENTREPRISES

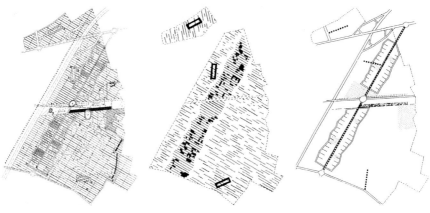

Site plan

Concert Hall and Exhibition Center
Rouen, France, 1998–2001

The motive of this project was to create a tool capable of fostering the economic expansion and cultural development of the Rouen district at the beginning of the 21st century. The site is an abandoned airfield well located at the entry to Rouen and less than an hour and a half by car from Paris. Dramatically visible from National Route 138, the 7000-seat concert hall, designed for rock concerts, political meetings and varied entertainments, the plaza and the 70,000-square-foot exhibition hall are placed on the 70 acres of a site structured by a grid of landscaping and lighting. The concert hall is designed to be visible with equal interest when heading to or away from Rouen on the highway.

The plaza opens towards the separate entrances of the exhibition hall and the concert hall. Openings in the structures allow the public to be welcomed generously into the spaces of the buildings without disrupting their structural logic.

The design of the buildings offers a degree of polyvalence. The exhibition hall permits diverse layouts so as to accommodate conventions for large crowds or trade fairs for limited professional groups. The concert hall provides for musical as well as sporting events, political conventions, summer schools, or theatrical shows. The 700-foot-long exhibition hall is conceived as a simple structure with a slightly vaulted roof, its horizontality contrasting with the curvature and guy-wired masts of the concert hall.

In the 350-foot-diameter concert hall, the typology of the classic concert facility has been transformed by developing a slight asymmetry in the audience seating. This asymmetry has the functional advantages of allowing the theater to be reconfigured into three smaller volumes and accommodating the off-center entry.

The structural system of the roof permits an economical long span as well as long-distance visibility when the three masts are illuminated on concert evenings. Tension cables hold the middle of the long spans, allowing a lighter truss system.

Acoustical concerns led to a complete double envelope surrounding the concert hall. The inner skin and concrete-stepped seating are doubled by the exterior skin, a broken torus of insulated corrugated metal. Located between the structural/acoustical envelope and the weather/security envelope is the "in-between" space of pedestrian circulation and gathering. Animated by the varied routes to the hall, its size makes it a major social space.

Torus plan

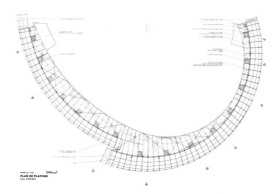

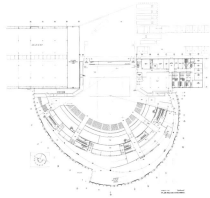

Ground level

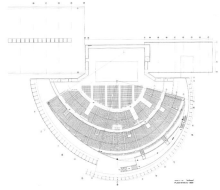

+9.50 m plan

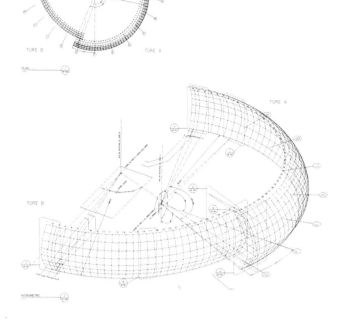

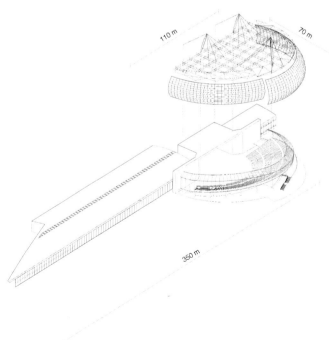

Axonometric

Entrance

Construction photograph

Exterior envelope

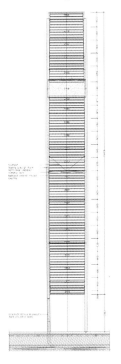

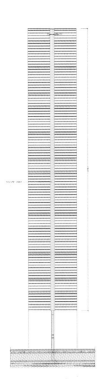

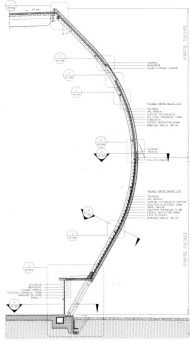

129

The building consists of two envelopes with movement in between them. The motion of people in crowds activates the interstitial space. Simple materials—metal, cast concrete and pre-fabricated concrete—were used, and the seats are purposefully transparent in order not to become "architecture." The ground is made out of natural concrete; galvanized metal shapes the details. The building is very minimalist, without the ideology associated with minimalism.

Movement in the in-between

Concert hall

Seating

Carnegie Science Center
Pittsburgh, Pennsylvania, 2000

It is said that today, scientific knowledge doubles every six months, but that this knowledge is largely additive and cumulative, rarely replacing or canceling earlier forms. In the same way, the new science center proposed in this competition entry would not "cancel" the older structure built several decades earlier, but rather encompass it, enlarging, extending and metamorphosing its contours. The project suggests that the existing floors could be retained while the old facade is partly removed to allow for the extension of exhibition galleries. The resulting new outer skin simultaneously provides protection against the weather and support for contemporary electronically-generated information.

The principle of an overall envelope circumscribing the existing floors while defining new spaces provides the basis of the project. The metal enclosure can be adapted to budgetary constraints, assuming either a cost-conscious "tight" fit or a "loose" one that provides additional square footage. Possible alternative layouts do not change the general concept, permitting the building to be extended in different directions on the site.

The arrangement of the new floor plates allows for two main display floors that each accommodate 35,000 square feet of continuous horizontal surface, permitting flexible subdivision according to curatorial needs. So as to encourage a range of different spatial sensations when the visitor moves through the building, the existing ramps were maintained but escalators also were added, along with a circular stair located at the junction between the existing and new floor plates. The result offers an exciting view over both the space and the scope of scientific knowledge that it contains.

Visible from a major vantage point along the river as visitors approach by car, the Science Center is intended to have a hypnotic presence, like a single stone on a beach or an object fallen from outer space.

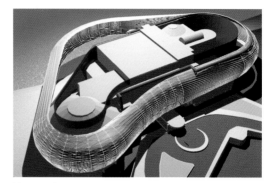
New envelope

Second floor exhibition space

New entrance hall

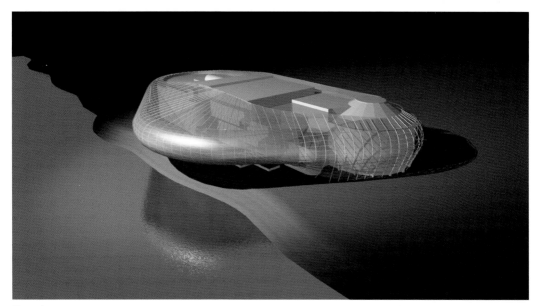

River view

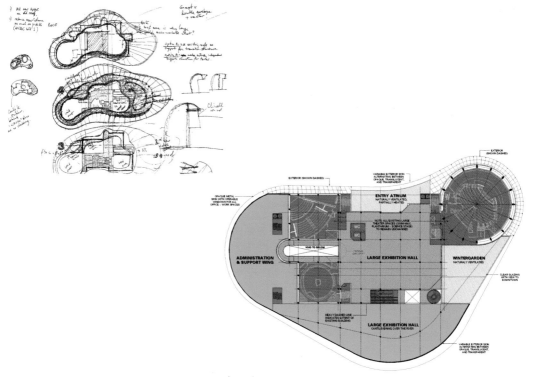

Conceptual plan

University of Cincinnati Athletic Center
Cincinnati, Ohio, 2001–

This athletic center proposed for the University of Cincinnati can be described as either a freestanding in-fill or a contextual free-form. Its unusual "boomerang" shape is designed to take advantage of the tight constraints of the site, resulting in dynamic residual spaces between the proposed curvilinear building, the existing stadium and arena, adjacent sports fields and the new recreation center. The building also offers spectacular views to and from the stadium.

A five-story atrium links the north and south street entrances and acts as a common space for all functions of the athletic center, from athletic offices on the top floor to training rooms below ground. Although athletes will be the principal users of the center, its auditorium, classrooms, University of Cincinnati Club, and practice fields will be shared with students and faculty from the greater university.

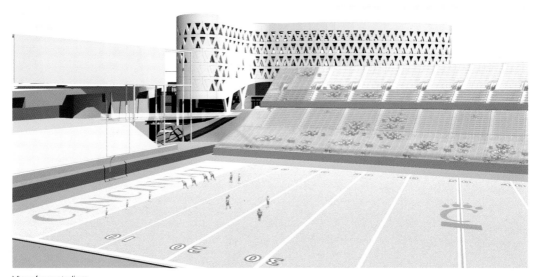

View from stadium

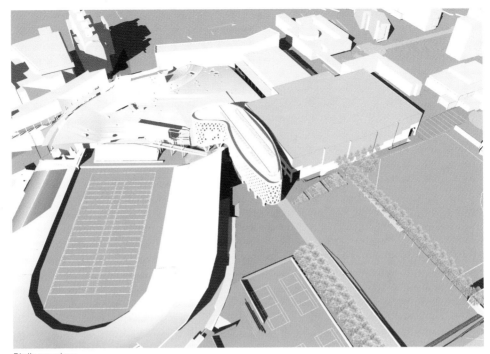

Bird's eye view

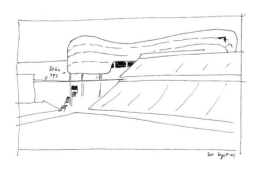

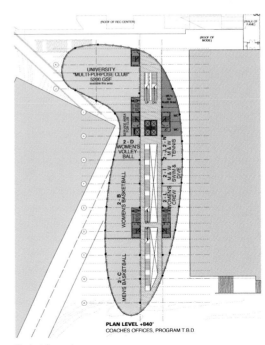

Typical floor plan

Vacheron Constantin Watch Factory and Headquarters

Geneva, Switzerland, 2001–

This building for the manufacturing and administrative headquarters of Switzerland's oldest watch making company developed from the image of a thin sheet with an elegant and delicately worked surface that can curve easily on itself. The surface that becomes the exterior is made of metal; the other surface, which will make up the interior, is doubled by wood veneer.

A light and slightly asymmetrical concrete supporting structure allows the metallic sheet to unroll, following the structure's geometry. The resulting space is sleek and precise on the exterior, warm and inviting on the interior. The space does not compose an enclosed object because the logic of the unrolling permits abundant light to enter on the north side and filtered light on the south, while opening to welcome workers and visitors to the facilities.

Beneath the underside of the metallic envelope is a parking lot that is sheltered by the building but also penetrated by natural light. Above it, the section reveals a calm and airy patio running through the building from east to west. The movement of the metallic sheet to form the building envelope ensures visual and functional continuity that extends from production to management and creation.

This continuity is repeated in the landscaping of the site, whose ordered plantings make the folded metallic sheet with its natural wood interiors appear as if placed inside a jewel box.

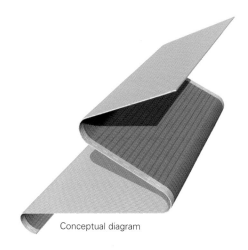

Conceptual diagram

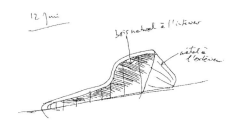

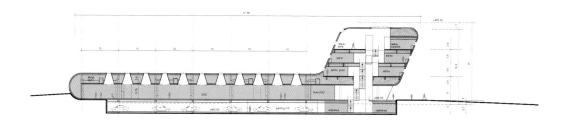

Section through ZAC

View from road

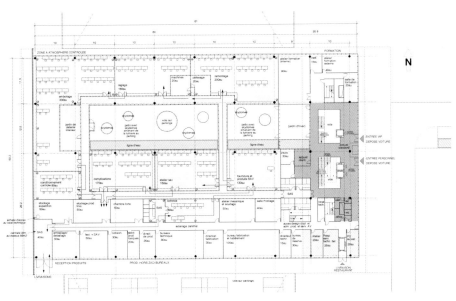

Ground level plan

Electronic Media Performing Arts Center, RPI
Troy, New York, 2000

As envisioned in this competition project, the Electronic Media Performing Arts Center is a multi-dimensional facility for the city as much as for the academic community. It is designed to be easily accessible and to extend the perception of the campus to its westernmost edge, which is strikingly visible from the Hudson River down below. The topography of the site allows the building to be entered at mid-level, leading to a three-dimensional experience as the visitor simultaneously sees above and below, left and right.

The building is read from outside to inside. Composed of five main materials—glass, metal, wood, light, and sound—it has outer and inner envelopes. The general concept of the building is of two envelopes with circulation passing between them. This simple notion allows maximum spatial flexibility inside the innermost envelope, while the glazed outer envelope or facade reveals the main circulation routes.

The double envelopes simultaneously provide a clear and powerful expression in the form of a glass cube and display dynamic activity behind the glass walls. The movement of visitors becomes a spectacle of its own. At night, the building becomes a shadow theater of real people and virtual images, providing a striking emblem of campus activities.

Each major programmatic entity, including theater, black box, recital hall and music practice rooms, is organized on its own level. Six main levels and four alternating mezzanine or intermediate levels allow a simple reading. All of the individual lobbies interact with the main circulation and social space of the building. The objective is identity and interaction.

Lobby stair

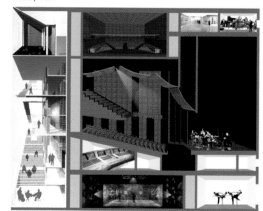

Section

View from below

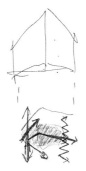

Double envelope with movement in-between

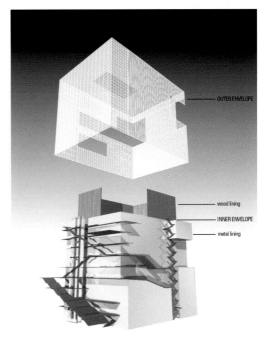

OUTER ENVELOPE

wood lining

INNER ENVELOPE

metal lining

Double envelope strategy

Museum for African Art
New York, New York, 2000–

An institution known for its creative scholarship and lively exhibition programs, The Museum for African Art plans to move from its current limited facilities to a new, free-standing building located on upper Fifth Avenue, on the south edge of Harlem. The building is designed as a new kind of museum that juxtaposes MAA's historic aim of exhibition with an increased focus on audience and accessibility. It combines traditional wood with a contemporary glass structure, and provides an emblem of access and participation to its visitors.

The building is intended to be both a resource and a stimulus. It includes flexible, dramatically-lit galleries characterized by an invisible integration of advanced technology, areas for education and research, multi-purpose social spaces and comfortable working environments for all staff. The entrance, retail area and café in the ground floor lobby offer the dynamism of an African bazaar, while a rooftop sculpture garden overlooks Central Park. Importantly, the museum is designed to suggest the creative multiplicity of African cultures while avoiding literal references.

Soaring glass walls on the perimeter of the structure afford views towards Central Park. In this manner, MAA will become the only museum on Fifth Avenue that exposes the park landscape through major views as one circulates through it, since escalators, elevators and stairs are all located on the periphery of the building.

Locating the fixed elements of circulation and servicing on the periphery of the floor plate allows maximum flexibility in the interior spaces. The structural system also permits three floors entirely without columns—the lobby, the large gallery for temporary exhibitions, and the "event-space" situated under the roof garden.

An important consideration in planning the museum is programmatic change and flexibility. The basis of the project is the glass enclosure, with the wood sanctum standing as the penetrable core of the museum experience. This principle provides a concept and identity for the museum that remains equally strong regardless of the size or scale determined by budgetary constraints. Thus, the glass can be 125 feet tall so as to abide by zoning regulations for the area surrounding the park, while the wood interior might be two, three or four stories high, without changing the general concept of the project.

Curtain wall detail

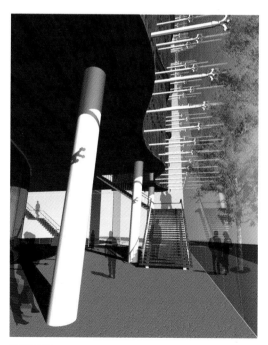
Entry view

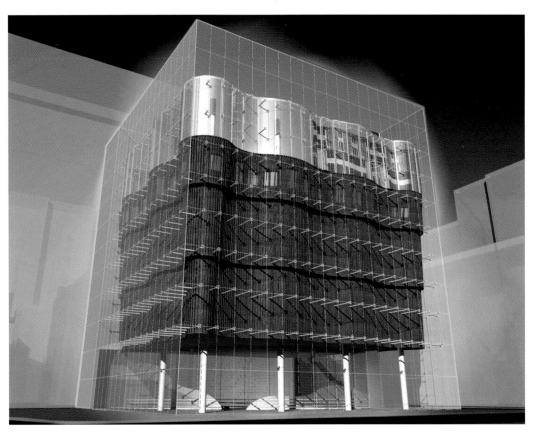

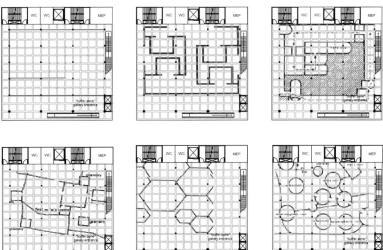

Flexible gallery arrangements based on African village plans

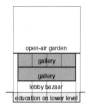
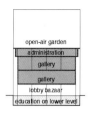

open-air garden
gallery
gallery
lobby bazaar
education on lower level

open-air garden
administration
gallery
gallery
lobby bazaar
education on lower level

open-air garden
administration
gallery
gallery
education
lobby bazaar

open-air garden
event space
administration
gallery
gallery
lobby bazaar
education on lower level

open-air garden
event space
administration
gallery
gallery
education
lobby bazaar

Flexibility in planning

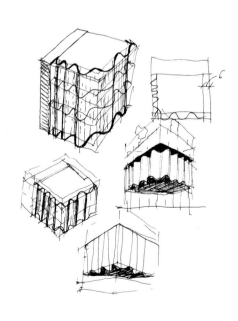

Concept collage

Section

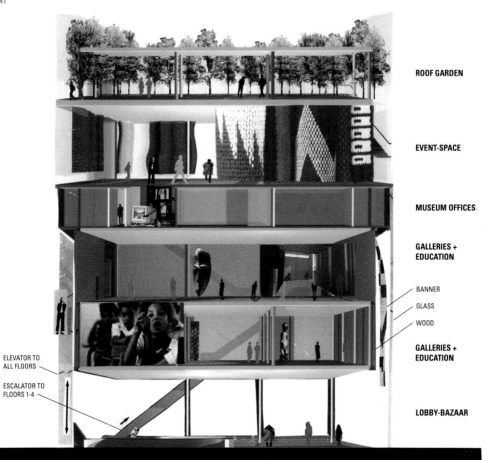

ROOF GARDEN

EVENT-SPACE

MUSEUM OFFICES

GALLERIES +
EDUCATION

BANNER

GLASS

WOOD

GALLERIES +
EDUCATION

ELEVATOR TO
ALL FLOORS

ESCALATOR TO
FLOORS 1-4

LOBBY-BAZAAR

145

New Acropolis Museum

Athens, Greece, 2001–

Three concepts turn the constraints of the site into an architectural opportunity, offering a simple and precise museum with the mathematical and conceptual clarity of ancient Greece.

A concept of light

More than in any other type of museum, the conditions animating the New Acropolis Museum revolve around light. Not only does daylight in Athens differ from light in London, Berlin or Bilbao; light for the exhibition of sculpture differs from that involved in displaying paintings or drawings. The NAM could be described as an anti-Bilbao. It is first and foremost a museum of natural light, concerned with the presentation of sculptural objects within it.

A movement concept

The visitor's route forms a clear three-dimensional loop, affording an architectural promenade with a rich spatial experience extending from the archeological excavations to the Parthenon Marbles and back through the Roman period.

Movement in and through time is a crucial dimension of architecture, and of this museum in particular. With over 10,000 visitors daily, the sequence of movements through the museum artifacts is conceived to be of utmost clarity.

A tectonic and programmatic concept

The base of the museum design contains an entrance lobby overlooking the Makriyianni excavations as well as temporary exhibition spaces, retail, and all support facilities.

The middle is a large, double-height trapezoidal plate that accommodates all galleries from the Archaic period to the Roman Empire with complete flexibility. A mezzanine welcomes a bar and restaurant with views towards the Acropolis, and a multimedia auditorium.

The top is the rectangular Parthenon Gallery around an outdoor court. The characteristics of its glass enclosure provide ideal light for sculpture, in direct view to and from the reference point of the Acropolis. The Parthenon Marbles will be visible from the Acropolis above. The enclosure is designed so as to protect the sculptures and visitors against excess heat and light. The orientation of the Marbles, which will be exactly as at the Parthenon, and their siting will provide an appropriate context for understanding the accomplishments of the Parthenon complex itself.

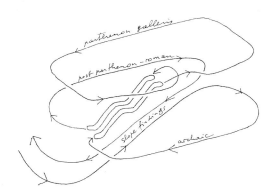

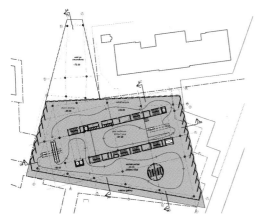

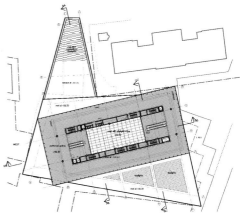

Plan at +92.5 m

Museu de Arte Contemporânea
São Paulo, Brazil, 2001–

Buildings can be introverted or extroverted. Stressing the privacy of esthetic experience, most museums tend to be the former. However, this new home for the Museu de Arte Contemporânea, which intends to move from its old location in a university to a dynamically growing section of São Paulo, provides an opportunity to develop a different type of museum, in which the city is an integral part of the museum experience.

The innovation of the new building is expressed by a simple formulation: the museum must not be just a container; it must also provide a context for the art of its time, setting it into relations both with the history of art and with the dynamics of the surrounding city. Much as the city has been an informing stimulus for 20th-century art, so the public, urban nature of experience should define the 21st-century museum.

The following terms describe the museum:
- It is vertical.
- It makes art and the city interact.
- Movement within it is visible from outside through a gallery ramp and a glass envelope.

In a way that is common to many new buildings in São Paulo, parking is located on the first four levels of the museum. A publicly-accessible covered lobby on the ground floor contains information services, a bookstore, and a ticket booth. The main lobby, however, is situated at the top of the building; the visitor ascends by elevator and then walks down along the external ramp to and through the galleries located on the floors below. The ramps provide striking vistas over the city. A restaurant and a sculpture garden are located on the roof.

Circulation through the galleries is provided by the ramps as well as by elevators and "short-cut" stairs connecting floors. Importantly, the ramps also serve as an "in-between" space, physically mediating between the collections and the city, and providing locations for exhibiting new art forms with public content and public modes of address.

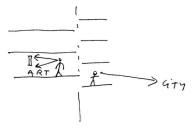

"The Museum is about art, but also about the city"

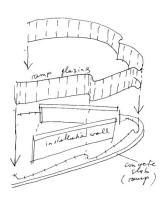

double envelope principle: ramp area acts as a protective buffer zone. With appropriate ventilation, it will minimize energy consumption in the galleries.

Exterior view

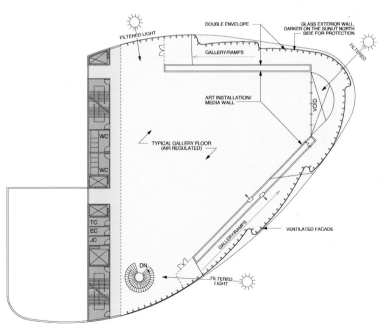

FILTERED LIGHT

DOUBLE ENVELOPE

GLASS EXTERIOR WALL,
DARKER ON THE SUNLIT NORTH
SIDE FOR PROTECTION

GALLERY/RAMPS

FILTERED

ART INSTALLATION/
MEDIA WALL

VOID

WC

TYPICAL GALLERY FLOOR
(AIR REGULATED)

WC

TC
EC
JC

GALLERY/RAMPS

VENTILATED FACADE

DN

FILTERED
LIGHT

Typical gallery plan

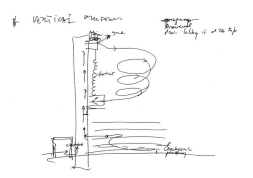

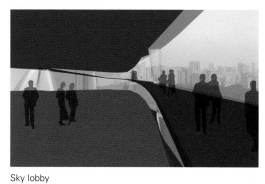

Sky lobby

Double envelope

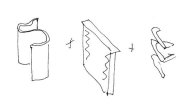

A RAMP GOES FROM BLACKOUT GALLERIES TO GALLERIES

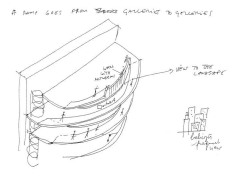

VIEW TO THE LANDSCAPE

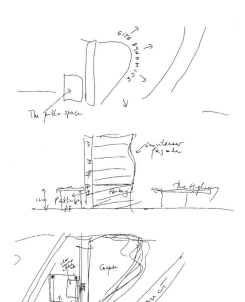

Night view

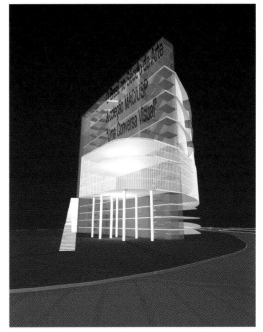

Night view of auditorium and signage

Postscript

Continuity
Giovanni Damiani

JACK (*to the first free man*): Soldier, is this the King's palace?
SECOND FREE MAN (*to the first*): Truth compels you to admit that we haven't got a king and so this building can't be the King's palace. We are the Free Men!
FIRST FREE MAN: Truth compels me?... Being Free Men, we shouldn't take orders even from truth itself.—Yes, mister foreigner, sir, this building is in fact the King's palace.
CORNHOLER: Oh goody goody! Here's a big tip for you—Jack![1]

In order to come to terms with Bernard Tschumi as an intellectual figure we should trace the geographic trajectory of his life, creating a thread that connects all the places in which he has resided. Without falling into biographical rhetoric, the image used by Tschumi in a prelude to an interview ("you might say I was born on the train between Paris and Lausanne"[2]) is in fact a metaphor for an existential condition of perpetual motion and compulsory cosmopolitanism.

The train, which strongly evokes the "first machine age", could be understood as a sort of home for a person born in 1944. What for the historical avant-garde was utopia, was a point of departure for the post-war generation. The train on which the young Tschumi "was born" is the materialization of the dream of the inhabitable machine, a dream that belonged, more than to anyone else, to Le Corbusier[3] and that became the starting condition for Tschumi's generation.

The young Tschumi lived in both Paris and Lausanne; he literally grew up among the drawings of his father's studio; and he traveled to America during his high school years. He crossed boundaries, flew over oceans, and at an early age fulfilled the destiny of his generation to "cross the threshold of the *urbs*" and cultivate the means by which a constantly expanding *civitas* begins to "coincide with the world." This cosmopolitanism would lead him to open a professional office with branches in New York and Paris.[4]

Tschumi's architectural training began at Zurich's ETH, where the Swiss modernist tradition was enriched by the pedagogical reforms introduced in Austin, Texas, and imported by Hoesli.[5] He worked in Zurich but also in Paris in the office of Candilis, Josic, and Woods during the galvanizing events of 1968. His decision to apprentice in this Parisian office signals a drastic break with the art of building solid and functional structures for a positivistic society, moving instead towards a society in a constant process of decomposition. Significantly, Tschumi's decision to work in Paris was not a definitive one[6]; in 1970, at age twenty-six, he moved to London to teach at the Architectural Association. It was his research that moved him,

Le Fresnoy National Studio for the Contemporary Arts, the in-between

155

that would not let him rest, and that could not "settle" in one place: that place was now London.

We should stop to reflect on what London represented at this time. London was the only large European capital that, although not without having paid a severe price, emerged victorious at the end of World War II.[7] It was the city that became the bridgehead for American production and for the pop culture generated by mass consumption. London was the city that fostered the conditions for a break with the Modern Movement and with the positivism of CIAM.

Since 1971 the AA had been directed by Alvin Boyarsky, a charismatic figure who encouraged open experimentation among its members. Recently, the AA has been celebrated and invested with a mythologizing aura primarily because of the utopian character of the so-called "radical" projects designed in its classrooms in the 1970s. However, its most significant contribution was the establishment of a safe haven in which young architects could work and experiment freely.[8] Along with Ron Herron, Peter Cook, and the first generation of the offspring of Team X, the AA welcomed a new generation, offering teaching opportunities over the decade to architects who included Leon Krier, Elia Zenghelis, Zaha Hadid, Bernard Tschumi, Nigel Coates, Peter Wilson, Charles Jencks, and Rem Koolhaas, among others.[9]

This freedom of research was often confused with the presumed "utopian" content of the architecture that was produced at the AA. In a literal sense, the term utopia denotes something that does not belong to any place, and many architects close to the "radical" groups always placed themselves outside any kind of *genius loci*. What must not be forgotten, however, is the slow but constant abandonment of the progressive vision that took place during the transition from radical research to the period in which the young teachers at the AA were expressing their maniacal interest in reality.

These "radicals" saw architecture not so much as a means of provocation than as a means of coming to terms with the new state of the world in the aftermath of the first machine age. The spirit of the times required that architecture occupy itself with building ships, airplanes, trains, and cars, thus fulfilling what Le Corbusier had envisioned during the golden age of the avant-garde. Architectural research now focused on the concept of motion, on the world outside the *urbs*,[10] on infrastructures and the places where networks and connections met; in this sense, the phenomenon of the "radicals" must be interpreted above all as the need to confront the new conditions of a city that was definitively becoming a metropolis. This was also the direction taken by the research carried out by the young Tschumi, one of whose earliest projects was *Do-it-yourself-city*.[11]

To paraphrase Tschumi's own words, the "fun palace" represents the contemporary home, and the "plug-in city" the modern-day *urbs*. There is nothing at all utopian about his premise: on the contrary, in examining these projects from a historical distance, they seem extremely concrete and feasible. Moreover, they seem to respond to their specific historical context, much as the projects of the Modern Movement brought attention to the crisis of their own day.

An entire generation was imbued with these important principles—a generation that understood that all inquiry must be directed toward the metropolis in order to be a part of its times, and that the metropolis was being built according to different rules, a fact which implied the radical and far-reaching revision of historical and cultural perspectives. It thus entailed a complete revision of a reality that had yet to be described and that demanded to be designed and built.

Just as the *Plan Voisin* must have seemed "excessive" for the society of the 1920s, the cultural project of confronting the uncontrollable aspects of the metropolis, and giving order to something that has none was in a sense "excessive" for its own time. Because the requirements were shifting, so were the instruments for describing, analyzing, and confronting reality. The famous slogan of 1968—"let's be reasonable, ask for the impossible"—truly embodies the "spirit of the times."

In confronting the present, it became necessary to recognize that the instruments of the first machine age had become obsolete. But in order to continue this struggle, it became necessary to break with a tradition that had become consolidated and no longer reflected the exigencies of mass culture. Tschumi's strategy was to begin from a description of the crisis:

Most people concerned with architecture feel some sort of disillusion and dismay because none of the early utopian ideals of the twentieth century has materialized, none of its social aims has succeeded. Blurred by reality, the ideals have turned into redevelopment nightmares and the aims into bureaucratic policies. The split between social reality and utopian dream has been total; the gap between economic constraints and the illusion of all-solving techniques absolute.[12]

The rupture with the avant-garde was a clean break. An unbridgeable distance arose between Tschumi's words and any attempt to give meaning to avant-garde practice. Paradoxically, this was the result of avant-garde practice and the desire to construct a different society which had been the primal impulse of the historical avant-garde. In turn, the historical avant-garde—once emptied of meaning following the failure of its ideology—became an aspect of the design process. This was true in the case of Tschumi, who re-read Joyce and Calvino in his classes, first at the AA and then at Princeton.[13] This was also true in the case of Koolhaas and Zenghelis, both of whom repeated, in postmodern fashion,[14] the Soviet experiments of Leonidov and the interpretative frenzies of Dalí and the Surrealists.

Elements that united the London generation of the 1970s were an indepth knowledge of Surrealism and an overwhelming interest in reality, aspects which, if combined, generated a sort of "Surrealist realism."[15] Although made up of autonomous personalities, the young group of teachers organized by Boyarsky shared the common philosophy that society had exploded into irretreivable pieces. There was no point in attempting to restore meaning to what Manfredo Tafuri called the avant-garde's "war talk."[16]

While Tafuri seemed to acknowledge that reality had complete domination over the battlefield,[17] this group of architects was paving new roads for a language that could not, and would not, exist in opposition to a possible "other," and instead sought to create a reality in dialectic with itself.

A dialectic that had no enemies among its opposition—and soon after would not even encounter opposition—is counterbalanced by the idea that in this struggle, one must fight the enemy that lies within.

The city and the society that had been founded on the dialectical values brought about by the French Revolution could no longer find enemies to oppose, while the metropolis that had originated from the values of mass culture still had vast front lines of conflict. The war was not over for the "step-children" of Team X. On the contrary, far from a group of heroic madmen conducting a private war whose outcome was already known, the children of this "Surrealist reality" sought new instruments in order to practice their profession on a global scale, and new ways to make architecture "dangerous" again.

From this perspective, one also should consider the rest of Tschumi's thoughts on the paradox of architecture:

Pointed out by critics who knew the limits of architectural remedies, this historical split has now been bypassed by attempts to reformulate the concepts of architecture. And in the process, a new split has appeared. More complex, it is not the symptom of professional naïvety or economic ignorance, but the sign of a fundamental question which lies in the very nature of architecture and of its essential element: space. By focusing on itself, architecture has entered an unavoidable paradox: the impossibility of questioning the nature of space and at the same time experiencing a spatial praxis.[18]

The short-circuit had been obvious and openly declared since the beginning. What changed radically was the decision to use this irrational energy, which could no longer be channeled by twentieth-century schemes, in the creation of alternative realities. This energetic metaphor also perfectly describes the research conducted in England before the 1970s whose legacy encompassed both Boyarsky's cultural project at the AA and its individual protagonists.

The dialectic on which that horizon of speculation had been based was now collapsed. The great trenches that had served as the last possible boundary between two polarities became a large Maginot line, inhabited only by ghosts and dense fragments of nostalgic memories of lost wholeness. While Aldo Rossi planned the Modena cemetery as a great and final enclosure to the collective memory of the orphans of Wholeness, elsewhere other challenges were being taken on: Rem Koolhaas' wall in *Exodus*, a polemical riposte to the megastructures popular at the AA, concealed within itself the metropolis, and "those who are fit enough to love it (the metropolis)" would be obliged to compete in order to become voluntary prisoners of the architecture. The new metropolitan avant-garde had come to understand that the conflict takes place inside, and that the wall is no longer a means of defense but rather a boundary that must be surpassed in order to reach a new condition: the place where things happen.

Crisis becomes both the highest criterion and the operative instrument; it is the principal resource for shaping reality, insofar as pure crisis is the reality of mass society. The themes of crisis that pervaded all the twentieth-century avant-garde movements had solidified and taken on a definitive shape; however, since this coagulation did not bring the hemorrhage to an end it demonstrated, instead, the futility of finding any cure.

During the solidification process, the coagulation of the flux of history produced new forms and sites for cultural debate; any attempt to employ positivist terminology in such instances could only produce monsters, destined to become styles. On the contrary, working with this coagulated material—and getting one's hands dirty with this surplus of history—created new scenarios for action. It would be an action that no longer yearned for the myth of Wholeness, and that in fact now openly opposed it. Why hold on to the desire for wholeness? Why hold on to longing for a compact city that no longer exists? Why be moved by the beauty of the purity of architecture of the Modern Movement?

The metropolis has revealed itself to be exquisitely beautiful and the departure offers new and even more extreme sensations; the Villa Savoye, now in ruins, has never been so beautiful. In one of his 1977 architectural manifestos Tschumi declared: "The most architectural thing about this building (the Villa Savoye) is the state of decay in which it is. Architecture only survives where it negates the form that society expects of it; where it negates itself by transgressing the limits that history has set for it."[19]

Tschumi's intuition is invested with extraordinary power and completely subverts any kind of formal discourse. It grows and corrodes the forms that are the means by which we come to terms with architecture; it is the mold that grows as the walls decay, the mold that renders the Villa Savoye part of the contemporary world, rather than a mere memory of a heroic past. The masses demand to live in the metropolis: angels compete to live in the "garbage can" of history,[20] and to take part in a metropolitan lifestyle that consists of movement and time.

Tschumi has chosen the theme of space as the battleground for his theoretical development. Space is not to be understood as a metaphysical place where forms are created in order to evoke memories, but rather as a site for experience; it is space in all its violence, the violence of reality. Here, Tschumi expounds on the theme of the violence of architecture:

By 'violence' I do not mean the brutality that destroys physical or emotional integrity but a metaphor for the intensity of a relationship between individuals and the spaces surrounding them. The argument is not a matter of style: modern architecture is neither more nor less violent than classical architecture, or than fascist, socialist, or vernacular variations. Architecture's violence is fundamental and unavoidable, for architecture is linked to events in the same way the guard is linked to the prisoner, the police to the criminal, the doctor to the patient, order to chaos. This also suggests that actions qualify spaces as much as spaces qualify actions; that space and action are inseparable and that no proper interpretation of architecture, drawing, or notation can refuse to consider this fact.[21]

And again:

Who will mastermind these exquisite spatial delights, these disturbing architectural tortures, the tortuous paths of promenades through delirious landscapes, theatrical events where actors complement decor? Who...? The architect? By the seventeenth century, Bernini had staged whole spectacles, followed by Mansart's *fêtes* for Louis XIV and Albert Speer's sinister and beautiful rallies. After all, the original action, the original act of violence—this unspeakable copulating of live body and dead stone—is unique and unrehearsed, though perhaps infinitely repeatable, for you may enter the building again and again. The architect will always dream of purifying the uncontrolled violence, channeling obedient bodies along predictable paths and occasionally along ramps that provide striking vistas, ritualizing the transgression of bodies in space. Le Corbusier's Carpenter Center, with its ramp that violates the building, is a genuine movement of bodies made into an architectural solid.[22]

According to Tschumi, violence is inherent in the architectural act and in the shaping of space. There is no such thing as innocence: anyone who practices architecture and designs spaces is forced to perform an act of violence, initially on the space itself and finally, on those who experience it.

The research that Tschumi conducted during these years is markedly French. His reading of Barthes's *Sade, Fourier, Loyola* seemed to permeate his thinking. More important than subjecting his texts to philological analysis in a search for origins and hidden citations[23] is the discovery of how these quintessentially French works also influenced the protagonists close to Tafuri's cultural project, as well as members of the Institute for Architecture and Urban Studies in New York.[24]

It is no coincidence that Tschumi, who taught at Princeton in 1976 and 1980, came into contact with the New York avant-garde, presented papers at the Institute for Architecture and Urban Studies, taught at the Cooper Union, and published his essay "Architecture and Transgression" in the journal *Oppositions*.[25]

Manfredo Tafuri published "L'Architecture dans le Boudoir: The Language of Criticism and the Criticism of Language" in the third issue of *Oppositions*.[26] This article, which would have a significant influence on American scholars and architects, suggested a possible convergence between contemporary Italian architecture and the neo-avant-garde New York Five. He elevated the works of James Stirling, Aldo Rossi and the New York Five as paradigms for the withdrawal of contemporary architects from the "sphere of the real" into the "universe of signs," the final symptom of a "diffused behavior whose intent is to regain the dimension of the object and its character as *unicum*, removing it from its economic and functional dimension... and placing it within the parenthesis of the flux of 'things' generated from the productive system." This withdrawal was referred to as "*architecture dans le boudoir*," a term derived from the Marquis de Sade's *La Philosophie dans le boudoir*. Tafuri insisted on the "Sadist understanding," according to which, in the erotic utopia of the boudoir, everything must refer exclusively and cruelly to sexuality. Borrowing from this concept, it became possible to assert that whenever the discipline of architecture was at stake, only the imposition of maximum terror and the "supreme constriction of geometrical structures" could effect a transgression of limits and absolute power.[27] For this reason, according to the Tafurian reading, the new "knights of purity" were compelled to seek the myth of autonomy:

Today, he who wishes to make architecture speak is thus forced to resort to materials devoid of all meaning; he is forced to reduce to degree zero every ideology, every dream of social function, every utopian residue.... In their own way, architects who from the late fifties until today have tried to reconstruct a universe of discourse for their discipline have felt obliged to resort to a new 'morality of restraint.' But their purism and their rigor are those of someone who is aware that he is committing a desperate action whose only justification lies in itself. The words of their vocabulary, gathered from the lunar wasteland remaining after the sudden conflagration of their grand illusions, lie precariously on that slanting surface that separates the world of reality from the solipsisms that completely enclose the domain of language.[28]

The subjects of the debate in Venice and New York were identical—crisis, language, and the possibility of architectural autonomy. The violence of the present, as demonstrated by the step-children of Team X, stood in contrast to the mnemonic oblivion of the Venice-New York axis.

The battleground was the same for all: New York. New York was many things at the same time: the economic capital of the western world; a city struggling to find its place in the complex American landscape of the 1970s while the country was still pursuing imperial objectives in Vietnam; a metropolis that anticipated changing fashions; and a great stage for show-business icons.

In opposition to the desperate "morality of restraint," the generation that was formed during the English Surrealist (neo)realism concluded that "asking for the impossible" was not only the sole sensible way to act, but also a feasible way to proceed in the new reality produced by the futility of trying to make sense out of history. The "extraordinary adventures of the meaningless" counteracted the failure of the Cartesian quest for laws and boundaries. The ultimate "crisis" of a normative reality brought about the rise of Surrealism.[29] Surrealist aspirations and procedures were now the only effective means of acting on reality. Rem Koolhaas spoke precisely to this point when discussing Dreamland:

In less than a decade they have invented and established urbanism based on the new technology of the Fantastic: a permanent conspiracy against the realities of the external world. It defines completely new relationships between *site, program, form,* and *technology*. The site has now become a miniature world; the program its ideology; and architecture the arrangement of the technological apparatus that compensates for the loss of physicality.[30]

Both Koolhaas and Tschumi addressed the problem of ideology's loss of meaning by using the power of Manhattan to launch an attack. American realism was the picklock used by Koolhaas (who recognized Manhattan to be more surreal than any kind of Surrealism and an avant-garde so fulfilled as to annihilate the avant-garde itself[31]) and by Tschumi, who responded to the "morality of restraint" with the "morality of excess" in the projects of *The Manhattan Transcripts*.

The Manhattan Transcripts was Tschumi's visiting card for his arrival in New York. Elaborated between 1976 and 1981 for a series of exhibitions, the work consists of a sequence of plates divided into four episodes: the park, the street, the tower, and the block.[32] The project is a true dismantling of the city, employing deconstructionist techniques similar to those used in cinematic media and literature. Taking as a starting point fragmentary sequences from films by Godard and other representatives of the avant-garde, Tschumi's plates describe the dematerialization of reality within the diagram and in an architecture that is forced to reconcile itself with the factor of time and to accept movement, the essential condition of metropolitan reality. What really interests Tschumi is the space generated by movement and life, and the distruptive effect of action on both architectural principles and the good intentions of architects.

Tschumi's acts of deconstruction in *The Manhattan Transcripts* free up movement through excess in response to the crisis intrinsic in the desperate "morality of restraint." There is an interesting dialectical dualism between the tragic, to which one must reply with restraint, and the seeming simplicity of the response of the Pop world, which counters the crisis of the West with the pure delirium of movement.[33]

To Tafuri's assertion that "today, he who wishes to make architecture speak is thus forced to resort to materials devoid of all meaning; he is forced to reduce to degree zero every ideology, every dream of social function, every utopian residue,"[34] the answer of the young architects formed under the wing of Team X seemed like a disarming opposition: ideology manufactured in the shape of a program.

While the Italians were obsessively pursuing a common groundwork, triggering an explosion of form now tragically exempt from any kind of responsibility, Pop culture, which had been conscious since its beginnings of the defeat of wholeness, accepted the notion that ideology might be part of the game, and included it in the notion of the program. Similarly, Tschumi wrote:

And vice versa: by ascribing to a given, supposedly 'autonomous' space a contradictory program, the space attains new levels of meaning. Event and space do not merge but affect one another. Similarly if the Sistine Chapel were used for pole-vaulting events, architecture would then cease to yield to its customary good intentions. For a while transgression would be real and all powerful. Yet the transgression of cultural expectations soon becomes accepted. Just as violent surrealist collages inspire advertising rhetoric, the broken rule is integrated into everyday life, whether through symbolic or technological motivations.[35]

The great values of Western culture formerly were employed as the essence of a program, as a functional set from which events might be generated. Now devoid of the ideological connotations that had inspired the design of utopias, anything could be assimilated by society, and at an ever more rapid pace.

In a discontinuous and non-linear history such as the one that developed after World War II, discontinuity and non-linearity serve as the means for establishing continuity with the struggle for modernity that had animated the era of the historic avant-gardes. It would be naïve to regard Tschumi's transformation into a key figure of the establishment as a product of the repudiation of youthful utopian visions: the transformation was a necessary and natural consequence of the earlier state, and ultimately a consequence of the London (neo)realist era that had its fruition in New York.

New York is the place where the transition from the '70s to the '80s occurred, where the new world order first manifested itself, and where postmodernism emerged as a condition. The metropolis finally became a desirable place, while the long trajectory of the historic avant-gardes came to an end. Tafuri cautioned that, "upon awakening, the world of fact takes on the responsibility of reestablishing a ruthless wall between the image of estrangement and the reality of its laws."[36] In New York, a new generation discovered new instruments with which to address the harsh laws of reality.

This "ruthless wall" emerges as the setting for a project cited on various occasions by Rem Koolhaas and also mentioned in *The Manhattan Transcripts*. While the Modern Movement tried to capture a potential "better world" inside that wall, the "Realist Surrealists" were only interested in what lay beyond it, which was not a better world but the world as it is. New York, with its rude manners and its externality to the dream of modernity cultivated in Europe, forms a perfect field of inquiry. This New York relinquished all possibility of stylistic refinement in order to become the capital of a harsher reality, extending from the sophistication of Miles Davis to the severity of the New Wave era metropolis where the soul has already been sold to the devil.[37] This is the city whose harsh reply to the bold linguistic experimentations of the New York Five was the cover of *Time* magazine in which Johnson described the style with which the Big Capital had chosen to represent itself after the post-Vietnam shift in economic strategies.

The path was laid: from the New York that sought the quality of the possible to the New York "without qualities" of Andy Warhol and Saturday Night Fever.

The desirability of the metropolis undermines the truculent language of the avant-garde, which remained somewhat like Dalí and his baguette as described in *Delirious New York*.[38] Meanwhile, New York's clubs exploded with energy.[39] At the turn of the decade, the question was how to become a star, how to exist in a reality that is irremediably patterned on the "society of the spectacle" and is without exit or dialectical alternative.

History proceeded with strict continuity. After the British (neo)realist era—described by early Pop Art, which was still examining the loss of values and searching for an existence without them—came the brutality of metropolitan reality, which no longer offered any way out. This was the New York that Tschumi confronted. He became part of an elite still in search of quality, frequenting the spaces of independent artists at the gallery Artists' Space, as well as the clubs of New York.[40]

Tschumi's work at that time was still positioned at the limit between art and the theoretical exploration of space. Here, Tschumi laid the foundation for his more properly architectural research, which started with the competition for the design of the Parc de La Villette. The steps leading towards a new architecture were evolving at the same pace that society was changing. For those who felt that they should and could live "without val-

163

ues," the design process was again possible. The discarded ideas left over from Surrealist realism served as the foundation for the strategy by which this new generation extricated itself from the checkmate of reality, as poignantly described by Tafuri. The Parc de la Villette became Tschumi's way of attacking reality.

With this 1982 project, Tschumi faced a competition that compelled him to put into practice his theoretical expertise. The competition notice drew the attention of numerous architects to a 125-acre territory, inciting a wide spectrum of solutions, from formal postmodernism to different stylistic interpretations and sophisticated linguistic research. Tschumi, in his first true attempt at architecture, won the competition after a neck-to-neck finish with OMA. A new generation rose to the attention of architectural debate; the time was ripe for the physical realization of theoretically-determined projects.

Tschumi imbued the park project with his concept of the city and materialized his concepts by establishing an interaction between grids and different superimposed systems. His goal was to generate spaces without necessarily establishing a dialogue among them. A project element, the "cinematic promenade," employs the montage techniques already explored in the *Transcripts* and in the academic exercises that Tschumi had assigned at the AA and Princeton. This promenade is contrasted to the point grid of *folies*, fragments that mark and organize the terrain.

The *folies*, the twenty-six pavilions housing restaurants, workshops and services, take their cue from Russian Constructivism with regard to their programs and their function as "social condensers," rather than with regard to their form. After all, these are *folies*. Form had now become but a simple game, even if rendered with a certain rigor. Tschumi's project for La Villette left no chance for dreams of form or utopias. The park's subject is the people who inhabit it, and the spatial relations that bind them together. Tschumi has written that

the point grid of *folies* constitutes the place of a new investment. The *folies* are new markings: the grafts of transference. These transference grafts allow access to space: one begins with an ambivalence toward a form in space that must be 'reincarnated.' The *folies* create a nodal point where symbol and reality permit the building of the imaginary by reintroducing a dialectic of space and time.

The movement of people through the large promenade holds together the great masses of the Zenith, the Grande Halle, and the Museum of Science and Technology; it is the experience of moving through the metropolis that creates space and relations among people and things. The project is constituted by an architecture generated by the social relations, movements, and spatial implications of those who experience it.[41]

Just as the great pendulum in Johnson's hands on the cover of *Time* represented the style chosen to represent the new economy, the operation put into play by Tschumi can be understood as a project that addresses the very society produced by the social crisis that spawned the movement towards postmodern style, while demonstrating the banality and uselessness of championing a specific style. The postmodern condition, which animates both the OMA and Tschumi project, does not require its own identifiable style; moreover, in order to display itself entirely, it is obliged to stave off any potential for formalism.

The inhabitants of the Parisian *banlieue*—a full-fledged melting pot—now bring the superimposed grids to life, generating spaces around the social condensers of the *folies*. The use of Constructivism should not be seen as a stylistic citation, but rather as a demonstration of the experience of modernity, transfigured according to the demands of a new society. It proclaims continuity with modernity's heroic age after emptying out the meaning of modernity itself. La Villette proclaims continuity with a history that no longer can be linear and continuous, but nevertheless can be utilized. It also provides a potential answer to the "crisis of values" that had instigated and inspired the historical avant-gardes. La Villette shows the conclusion of the crisis and the possibility of living in events[42]—*in the universe of facts*, where the analysis developed by Tafuri stops. La Villette is a cry of relief that responds to the crisis by asking, "So what?" Haven't all the avant-gardes debated this topic? Aren't we the undeniable product of the crisis?

From this perspective it was possible to design the Library of France, an institution that can be seen as a metaphor for Western culture, surmounted by a running track, as Tschumi did in 1989. As before, the project resulted from an amalgamation of techniques. Tschumi attempted to unite the supreme cultural institution with something popular, combining different programs through intersection. Unlike Perrault's winning project, Tschumi's project is integrated with the Parisian skyline, and proposes a serial layout for the internal distribution of books. Space would have been transformed by the movement of people through the various halls, creating circuits; in turn, the circuits of culture, books, and data were juxtaposed with the athletic track, the true *circus maximus* of modern times. The intellectual of the new era, Tschumi hypothesized, is also an athlete—an actualized *Übermensch*.

Within the context of this perfect continuity with our surreal reality, it should come as no surprise that in 1988 Tschumi was asked to direct Columbia University's Graduate School of Architecture. This signified that reality had become aware of the status quo, namely, that Surrealism had come into power and that it was no longer possible to distinguish normalcy from its opposite, or the whole from the deconstructed.

The world follows its course; all that is meant to be, happens. Everything transpires in a space that is negotiated and uncertain, a space that becomes the new territory for architecture. Locations become conflated, and what ought to be the ultimate location, the king's palace, is now a home like any other. At the same time, anyone who understands the mechanisms and rules of a society that has already exploded, and who realizes that the revolutionary era of the 1960s was merely an attempt to rearticulate turning points that had already taken place in reality, knows that any home can now become the king's palace.

The journey to the end of the night that had enabled architecture to actualize the most extreme consequences of the loss of meaning and the confusion of the order of things had now been fulfilled, and architects like Tschumi recognized the dawn of a new era.

In the project for Le Fresnoy, completed in 1997, Tschumi's references to the tragic nature of Piranesi's *Prisons* were liberal and ludic. The project for a contemporary art center, designed through the renovation of, and addition to, a 1920s entertainment complex, was achieved by means of a great, expansive cover. Underneath this large metal roof structure, the external restoration of the old buildings was limited to the application of a fresh coat of paint and a minimum of maintenance.[43]

This great umbrella, a kind of a container for other containers, permits the annexation of a number of service areas, facilities, and catwalks to its own structure. Remarkably, if we travel through these spaces we sometimes discover that they lead to nowhere, to nothing. Walking on the pathways suspended from the overarching umbrella structure, we can sit on the steps of a small open-air theater, also suspended, from which we can contemplate the roofs of the industrial buildings below or people moving along the other pathways suspended between the old roofs and the great cover. People, who in their motion are living the metropolitan condition, both experience space and create fluxes—fluxes that have become nothing more than ends in themselves. All is in flux, and flux creates more flux. Commodities are derived from other commodities, and space is created out of space.

As one descends one of the small spiral staircases in this "in-between" space, it sometimes becomes necessary to ascend once again upon realizing that it leads nowhere. We find ourselves imprisoned in a Piranesian game of spatial perversion. The large staircase giving access to the system of suspended spaces in the interstices between the roof cover and the buildings underneath has a double set of steps: to one side are steps on a human scale, while to the other are steps whose scale reminds us of the mythological age of the giants who once tortured us, and of the space experienced by a man trapped in Piranesi's *Prisons*. Piranesi, the "wicked architect" who, according to Tafuri, instigated the apocalypse of the avant-garde,[44] is employed with absolute (a-)normality.

1 Alfred Jarry, *Ubu Enchained*, trans. S.W. Taylor, New York 1969, p. 135.

2 Y. Futagawa, "Interview with Bernard Tschumi," in *GA Document Extra*, 10, 1997.

3 This was certainly not only Le Corbusier's dream; he, like many others, was responding to an exigency of his own era. During his entire intellectual career, Le Corbusier continued to question the significance and function of the house. His response was the airplanes, cars, and ships in *Towards a New Architecture*. This subject was discussed in Massimo Cacciari's paper delivered at the fourth conference in honor of Manfredo Tafuri at the Department of History of Architecture at the Istituto Universitario di Architettura in Venice on February 23,1998, published in *Casabella* (662/663, December 1998/January 1999, p. 2-5): "What is really today's house? The means by which it is possible to proceed, to pave one's way. Thucydides used to say: the ship is the home of the Athenian. The means that goes beyond the boundaries of the *urbs*, the instrument through which the *civitas* evolves and becomes one with the world: here is where we live.... We live in the means. The home, when not an idol... is the bridges, harbors, streets, the machines which go through them, the information which circulates therein." (p. 3)

4 In interviews, Tschumi has insisted that his main office is neither in New York or Paris, but that his offices in each of these two cities are complementary to each other and conceived of as one unit. This is noteworthy since Tschumi's generation seems to have embodied certain ideals that later became the backbone of globalization. Paradoxically, very little of what was proposed during the 1960s protests has survived in today's society, while the laws and nature of world economic globalization were derived precisely from this moment of discontinuity.

5 Cf. Alexander Caragonne, *Texas Rangers*, MIT Press, Cambridge, MA 1995. Caragonne's study, apart from offering an exhaustive history of the Austin school, also pinpointed influence that it had over the radical transformations that occured in American architecture during the 1960s and 1970s. It is interesting to analyze Colin Rowe as a central figure of this school. Drawing on his studies with Wittkower, Rowe sought harmony and proportions for contemporary architecture—a cultural project opposed to that of the Independent Group, from which developed Team X's division from CIAM. Rowe was Peter Eisenman's teacher at Cornell University as well as the mentor for the New York Five and the "white" American current, with whom Tschumi and other "step-children" of Team X would come into contact in New York in the 1970s.

6 Louis Martin emphasizes Tschumi's desire not to restrict himself to being French in his essay "Transpositions: On the Intellectual Origins of Tschumi's Architectural Theory," in *Assemblage*, 11, 1998, p. 32.

7 London had both Wittkower at the Warburg Institute and Banham, whose work on the reform of teaching methods through a reinterpretation of avant-garde movements formed the subject of a series of conferences at the Institute of Contemporary Arts. The two individuals who were destined to become possible epigones of subsequent architectural culture were both living in post-World War II London. In the same city, continuity with avant-gardes in the historical break co-existed with historical continuity in the break with modernity.

8 An interesting panorama can be found in *The Architectural Review*, 1040, October 1983, which is dedicated entirely to pedagogy and the AA. The issue includes an interesting interview with Boyarsky.

9 Rem Koolhaas was the first to depart for the United States; as a student, he was already openly polemical concerning the architecture taught and practiced at the AA. See Patrice Goulet, "La Deuxième chance de l'architecture moderne: entretien avec Rem Koolhaas," in *L'Architecture d'aujourd'hui*, 238, April 1985.

[10] This is the meaning of living in the train in the passage, and Cacciari's words, previously cited, come back to us: "[Editor's note: He is talking of Socrates.] In the great apologies for philosophy, this seems to be the ultimate end: every dimension 'de economica,' anything having to do with the *oikos* (including the daily affairs of the polis, since they pertain to economy) are research traps for philosophers. The house constitutes the aporia of Eros—where its own *poros* is interrupted, where its own *skepsis* is interrupted. If to philosophize is to continue indefatigably on one's own path—moreover, to always produce it by means of the same research—then, how can a philosopher be also... an inhabitant? Is it possible to "inhabit" roads, boundaries, passages, and distances?" (p. 2-3) Again: "The places of our non-being are but passing; this is what the architect should plan-design, powerful enough to renounce the *mimesis* of idea. *Passagenwerke* should be his buildings, manifestations of the impossibility of living. *Atopia* is its place par excellence, since each place (each genius loci) should be for him but an element of a network without confines in which what is produced, exchanged, and communicated become intertwined." (p. 3) In the appendix of the Italian edition of Rem Koolhaas's *Delirious New York*, Milan 2001, p. 294, Marco Biraghi invests the Manhattan skyscraper with the role that the *Passagenwerke* had in Benjamin's Paris.

[11] "Do-It-Yourself-City," in *L'Architecture d'aujourd'hui*, 148, February-March 1970, p. 98-105, is Tschumi's first work, written in collaboration with Fernando Montés.

[12] Bernard Tschumi, *Questions of Space: Lectures on Architecture*, Architectural Association, London 1990, p. 12. This work was first published in *Studio International*, September/October 1975.

[13] See *The Architectural Review*, 1040, October 1983, p. 60-63.

[14] The term "postmodern" used throughout this essay has no connection whatsoever to the style generated, or degenerated, from the euphoria that followed the dismantling of society produced by the French Revolution. My understanding of the term is identified with Lyotard's elaboration of it in his well-known book, *The Postmodern Condition: A Report on Knowledge*, Minneapolis 1984: "The object of this study is the condition of knowledge in the most highly developed societies. I have decided to use the word postmodern to describe that condition. The word is in current use on the American continent among sociologists and critics; it designates the state of our culture following the transformations which, since the end of the nineteenth century, have altered the game rules for science, literature, and the arts. The present study will place these transformations in the context of the crisis of narratives." (p. xxiii)

[15] "Surrealist Realism" denotes a strong interest for a more complex reality: a hyper-reality of sorts, which requires a series of new instruments in order to be understood. These instruments include the surreal, the lucid delirium, the "more-than-real," and work with objects that can be dismantled from the revision of surrealist practices. The generation in question is not delirious simply because it wants to abandon history's trails and the rules of harmony and proportion, but because it has to continue to follow a reality that is no longer constructed according to rules of harmony.

[16] Manfredo Tafuri, "Le avventure del linguaggio, ovvero *la guerra è finita*," in *Five Architects* N.Y., Officina, Rome 1981.

[17] "The war has ended, but with a checkmate imposed on the enemy. All that remains to be done is to declaim with affectionate irony, with a nostalgia barely disguised, the verses of the Marseillaise badly decomposed and frozen. (Is freezing not supposed to be a safe form of conservation?)" writes Tafuri at the end of his work *Le ceneri di Jefferson*. See Tafuri, *The Sphere and the Labyrinth*, Cambridge, MA 1987, p. 369.

[18] Tschumi, *Questions of Space, op. cit.*, p. 12.

[19] Cf. in this volume p. 28-31.

[20] The angels are the figures rushing towards Manhattan in Koolhaas and Zenghelis's project, *Exodus, or the Voluntary Prisoners of Architecture*. They are clearly visible in the color plates in Jeffrey Kipnis, *Perfect Acts of Architecture*, The Museum of Modern Art and the Wexner Center for the Arts, New York 2002, p. 20.

[21] Bernard Tschumi, "Violence and Architecture," in *Architecture and Disjunction*, MIT Press, Cambridge, MA 1996, p. 122.

[22] *Ibid.* p. 125-6.

[23] On the French foundation of Tschumi's theoretical notions and on Barthes's influence rather than Derrida's *Tel Quel*, see Louis Martin, "Transpositions: On the Intellectual Origins of Tschumi Architectural Theory," in *Assemblage*, 11, 1998, p. 23-35. Tschumi's relations with French intellectuals and his attempt to redefine architectural discipline in the light of recent work are immediate and obvious and must be viewed carefully. Martin's article scrutinizes the texts employed by Tschumi to construct his theories and comes to important conclusions regarding Tschumi's use of "architectural translation." It is interesting to note that while many architects have made use of Derrida incessantly, making him one of the most sought after and quoted scholars of the last decades, Tschumi's work at La Villette was the subject of Derrida's own interesting study, "Point de folie - maintenant l'architecture," in Bernard Tschumi, *La case vide*, Architectural Association, London 1986.

[24] The Institute of Architecture and Urban Studies (IAUS), founded by Peter Eisenman along with Kenneth Frampton, Mario Gandelsonas, and Diana Agrest, represents a key moment in the history of architectural theory of the 1970s. The journal associated with this school, *Oppositions*, became an important forum for intellectual exchange. Animated by the position of the "Whites", who took their name from the search for the lost purity of the Modern Movement, *Oppositions* provided an opportunity for an analysis of a crisis that was to be solved according to Progressivist solutions. It is worth noting that this cultural experiment ended with a monographic issue on Aldo Rossi. The attempt to explore possible solutions for linear continuity with the Modern Movement came to a standstill with the sheds drawn by Aldo Rossi for the cover of issue no. 26. An escape into personal memory seemed the only way out for those who still dreamt of opposition, those who still believed in the possibility of linear continuity with the history of the avantgarde movements.

[25] Bernard Tschumi, "Architecture and Trangression," in *Oppositions*, 7, 1976.

[26] Tafuri, "L'Architecture dans le Boudoir: The Language of Criticism and the Criticism of Language," in *Oppositions*, 3, 1974.

[27] Tafuri's Foucauldian reading is contemporary with Bernardo Tschumi's essays. "The Architectural Paradox" and "Questions of Space" in *Studio International*, London, September/October 1975, and also in "Architecture and Transgression," in *Oppositions*, 7, 1976. The essays, however, have somewhat opposite destinies.

[28] Tafuri, "L'Architecture dans le Boudoir," in *The Sphere and the Labyrinth, op. cit.*, p. 267-8.

[29] This brings to mind Antonioni's *Blow-up*, a film centered on the British avantgarde, that opens with a protesting crowd and ends with a surreal tennis match played without a ball. The big "umpire" chairs in the game area of the park at La Villette can be understood as a materialization of the notion that the only rules that are still valid are those of games. These are games in which the referees do not have before them a delineated field, but instead a series of events positioned on a terrain covered with anti-Cartesian irregularities, a fitting metaphor for contemporary society. Tschumi makes reference to *Blow-up* in the chapter named "Park" in *The Manhattan Transcripts*, in which he evokes the disappearance of the subject proposed by Antonioni.

[30] Rem Koolhaas, *Delirious New York*, *op. cit.*, p. 56.

[31] See Koolhaas' treatment of Dalí's arrival in New York in *Delirious New York*, *op. cit.*, p. 243, and the entire chapter "Europei: Attenti! Dalí e Le Corbusier conquistano New York," p. 223-261.

[32] The projects for *The Manhattan Transcripts* were exhibited for the first time at the Artists Space in April 1978 and the following year in the New Gallery at the AA in an expanded form.

[33] In British utopian era, "Fun" became the English version of the Situationist "détournement." For Debord and the children of May 1968, the loss one's sense of direction in the metropolis embodies the political project which will become fossilized in Britain once it comes in contact with the market of post-war capitalism. Dance, movement, and serious games are the elements employed by Tschumi in the *Transcripts* in order to set off the mechanism for the decomposition of Manhattan. In 1960s London, wandering without a goal or a political project became a part of youth culture, the subject and industry of fun, as demonstrated by Paola Colaiacomo and Vittoria Caratozzolo. This crazed amusement is "fun": the practice of excess as an attack towards the "morality of restraint." Paola Colaiacomo and Vittoria Caratozzolo, *La Londra dei Beatles*, Editori Riuniti, Rome 1996.

[34] Manfredo Tafuri, "L'Architecture dans le Boudoir", in *The Sphere and the Labyrinth, op. cit.*, p. 267.

[35] Bernard Tschumi, *Architecture and Disjunction, op. cit.*, p. 130.

[36] Manfredo Tafuri, *The Sphere and the Labyrinth, op. cit.*, p. 303

[37] "I sold my soul, must be saved / Gonna to take a walk down Union Square / You never know who you're gonna find there / You gotta run, run, run." The Velvet Underground, "Run Run Run," in The Velvet Underground & Nico, Verve 1967.

[38] Rem Koolhaas, *Delirious New York, op. cit.*, p. 243.

[39] According to Andy Warhol, the key to Studio 54's success was that it was a dictatorship outside and a democracy inside. At 54 everyone who made it in was equally a star and thus equally unimportant. Andy Warhol, *La cosa più bella di Firenze sono i McDonald's*, Stampalternativa, Rome 1994.

[40] On the Artists Space and Tschumi, see *Skyline*, May, 1979 which features Tschumi's article on his theoretical works and in particular on *Staircase for Scarface*, a 1979 installation for Castle Clinton in central Manhattan.

[41] Bernard Tschumi, *Architecture and Disjunction, op. cit.*, p. 179. The chapter "Madness and the Combinative" first appeared in *Precis*, Columbia University Press, New York 1984.

[42] The 'event' is the foundation for all of Tschumi's theoretical speculations—from *The Manhattan Transcripts*, to the famous slogan about there being no architecture without events, to the two thick volumes of Event-Cities, which gather Tschumi's projects and were published by MIT Press in 1994 and 2000.

[43] For Le Fresnoy, see: Bernard Tschumi, Joseph Abram, "The Architectural Project of Le Fresnoy," in *Tschumi Le Fresnoy: Architecture in/between*, The Monacelli Press, New York, 1999, and the multi-author volume, *Tschumi une architecture en project Le Fresnoy*, Centre Georges Pompidou, Paris 1993, containing a recent series of interesting essays.

[44] See Tafuri's essay on Piranesi that starts the chapter "Prelude: apocalipsis cum figuris," in *The Sphere and the Labyrinth, op. cit.*, p. 25-54.

Giovan Battista Piranesi,
etching from *Carceri
d'invenzione*

Appendix

Biography

Bernard Tschumi is an architect and educator. A permanent United States resident who holds both French and Swiss nationalities, Tschumi studied in Paris and at he Federal Institute of Technology (ETH) in Zurich, Switzerland, from which he received his degree in 1969. He taught at the Architectural Association in London (1970-79), the Institute for Architecture and Urban Studies in New York (1976), Princeton University (1976 and 1980), and the Cooper Union (1981-83). He has been Dean of the Graduate School of Architecture, Planning and Preservation at Columbia University in New York from 1988 to 2003.

First known as a theorist, he exhibited and published *The Manhattan Transcripts* (1981) and wrote *Architecture and Disjunction*, a series of theoretical essays (MIT Press, 1994). In 1983, he won the prestigious competition to design the Parc de la Villette, a 125-acre public park containing dramatic buildings, walkways, bridges, and gardens at the northeast edge of Paris. Tschumi established his Paris office in 1983, followed by the New York office in 1988. Completed projects include Le Fresnoy National Studio for Contemporary Arts in Tourcoing, France; Columbia University's Lerner Hall Student Center; Marne-La-Vallée School of Architecture, Paris; the Interface Flon, a bus, train, and subway station and pedestrian bridge in Lausanne, Switzerland; a Concert Hall and Exhibition Center in Rouen, France; and the Florida International University School of Architecture in Miami, Florida. Tschumi was one of three international finalists selected by The Museum of Modern Art in New York in 1997 to design its new expansion. He is currently designing The Museum for African Art in New York, the New Acropolis Museum in Athens, and the Museum of Contemporary Art in Sao Paolo, which were all winning entries to international competitions, as well as buildings in Cincinnati, Ohio, and Geneva, Switzerland. Tschumi is a member of the Collège International de Philosophie in France and the recipient of many distinguished honors, including the Légion d'Honneur and the Ordre des Arts et Lettres. He was awarded France's Grand Prix National d'Architecture in 1996, as well as awards from the American Institute of Architects and the National Endowment for the Arts.

Books by or on Bernard Tschumi

• Jeffrey Kipnis, Todd Gannon, *Source Books in Architecture 3: Bernard Tschumi/Rouen Concert Hall*, Princeton Architectural Press, New York 2003
• Bernard Tschumi Urbanistes Architectes (BTuA), *Virtuæl*, BTuA/Actar Barcelona 2003
• Bernard Tschumi, Matthew Bernam, eds., *INDEX Architecture: a Columbia Book of Architecture*, MIT Press, Cambridge, MA and London 2003
• Michele Costanzo, *Bernard Tschumi. L'architettura della disgiunzione*, Testo e Immagine, Turin 2002
• Bernard Tschumi, Hugh Dutton, *Glass Ramp/Glass Wall*, Architectural Association, London 2001
• Bernard Tschumi, *Event-Cities 2*, MIT Press, Cambridge, MA and London 2000
• Joseph Abram et al., *Le Fresnoy: Architecture In/Between*, The Monacelli Press, New York 1999
• "Bernard Tschumi", *GA Document Extra*, Tokyo, 1997
• Bernard Tschumi, *Architecture and Disjunction: Collected Essays 1975-1990*, MIT Press, Cambridge, MA and London 1994 (Fourth printing, 1998)
• Bernard Tschumi, *Event-Cities*, MIT Press, Cambridge, MA and London 1994 (Fifth printing, 1999)
• Joseph Abram et al., *Tschumi, une architecture en projet: Le Fresnoy*, Editions du Centre Pompidou, Paris 1993
• Bernard Tschumi, *Questions of Space*, Architectural Association Publications, London 1990
• Bernard Tschumi, *Cinegramme Folie: le Parc de la Villette*, Princeton Architectural Press/Champ Vallon, Princeton and Paris 1987
• Bernard Tschumi, *La Case Vide, Folio VIII*, Architectural Association Publications, London 1986
• Bernard Tschumi, *The Manhattan Transcripts: Theoretical Projects* Academy Editions/St. Martin's Press, New York and London 1981 (Reprinted in expanded version, 1994)

Selected one-person exhibitions

2003
New Acropolis Museum, Onassis Foundation, New York
2003
Virtuael, La Galerie d'Architecture, Paris
1997
Architecture In/Of Motion, NAI, Netherlands Institute of Architecture, Rotterdam
1994
Architecture and Event, The Museum of Modern Art, New York
1988
Disprogramming, Gallery MA, Tokyo
1987
Selected Work, Skala Gallery, Copenhagen
1987
Disjunctions, Aedes Gallery, Berlin
1986
Parc de la Villette, Architectural Association, London
1985
Parc de la Villette, Max Protetch Gallery, New York
1985
From The Transcripts to La Villette, Institut Francais d'Architecture, Paris
1985
Selected Work, Milan

Triennale, Milan
1984
Selected Work,
IBA Internazionale
Bauanstellung, Berlin
1981
*The Manhattan Transcripts -
Part 4*, Max Protetch
Gallery, New York
1980
*The Manhattan Transcripts -
Part 3*, P.S.1, Long Island
City, New York
1979
Architectural Manifestos II,
Architectural Association,
London
1978
Architectural Manifestos I,
Artists Space, New York

Selected group exhibitions
2002
Now, Venice Biennale,
Venice
2002
Folds, Boxes, and Blobs,
The Museum of Modern
Art, San Francisco
2002
*Perfect Acts of
Architecture*, AXA Gallery,
The Museum of Modern
Art, New York
2001
*Perfect Acts of
Architecture*, The Wexner
Center, The Ohio State
University, Columbus
2001
EXPERIENCES, Museu
d'Art Contemporani de
Barcelona, Barcelona
2000
*City: Less Esthetics, More
Ethics*, Venice Biennale,
Venice
1999
The Un-Private House, The
Museum of Modern Art,
New York
1998
*Rethinking the Modern:
Three Proposals for*

*The Museum of Modern
Art*, The Museum
of Modern Art, New York
1996
Living Bridges, Royal
Academy of Art, London
1996
Venice Biennale, French
Pavilion, Venice
1995
Light Construction, The
Museum of Modern Art,
New York
1994
L'objet de l'architecture,
CCC, Tours
1993
Recent Acquisitions, Centre
Pompidou, Paris
1992
Theory + Experimentation,
Royal Institute of British
Architects, London
1988
Architecture in New York,
Deutsches
Architekturmuseum,
Frankfurt-am-Main
1988
*Deconstructivist
Architecture*, The Museum
of Modern Art, New York
1984
Follies, Leo Castelli Gallery,
New York
1983
Parc de la Villette, Centre
Pompidou, Paris
1982
Documenta, Kassel
1981
Architecture: Sequences,
Artists Space, New York
1980
L'Urbanité, Paris Biennale,
Centre Pompidou, Paris
1979
Urban Places, Cooper-
Hewitt Museum,
New York
1975
*A Space: A Thousand
Words*, Royal College of
Art, London

Project Credits
• Parc de la Villette
Competition: Bernard
Tschumi, Luca Merlini,
Alexandra Villegas,
Luca Pagnamenta, Galen
Cranz, Phoebe Cutler,
William Wallis, Jon Olsen,
Thomas Balsley; *project*:
Bernard Tschumi, Jean-
François Erhel, Ursula Kurz,
Alexandra Villegas,
Luca Merlini, Christian
Biecher, Marie-Line
Luquet, Neil Porter,
Steve McAdam, Luca
Pagnamenta, Jean-Pierre
Nourry, Didier Pasquier,
Renzo Bader
Consultants: Planning: Colin
Fournier; SETEC-TP;
Structural (bridge and
gallery structures): Peter
Rice (RFR) with Hugh
Dutton
**• New National Theatre
and Opera House**
Bernard Tschumi, Luca
Merlini, Christian Biecher,
Patrick Winters, Martyn
Wiltshire, Alexandra
Villegas
• 17th Street Loft
Bernard Tschumi
**• Kansai International
Airport**
Bernard Tschumi, Koichi
Yasuda, Robert Young,
Mark Haukos, Frazer
Gardiner, Gilbert Schafer,
Mehrdad Hadighi, Hugh
Dutton (RFR), Stan Allen,
Luca Merlini, Ursula Kurz,
Christian Biecher
**• Interface/Bridge-
City/Metropont/CAPC
(Center for Contemporary
Visual Arts)**
Bernard Tschumi
and Luca Merlini.
Competition: Bernard
Tschumi, Luca Merlini,
Christian Biecher, Philippe
Gavin, Ursula Kurz,

Emmanuel Ventura;
CAPC: Bernard Tschumi,
Robert Young, Jim Sullivan;
Metropont: Bernard
Tschumi, Luca Merlini,
Richter + Gut, Architram,
Robert Young, Véronique
Descharrières, Emmanuel
Ventura, Marc Sautier, Hugh
Dutton (RFR);
Interface: Bernard Tschumi,
Luca Merlini, Emmanuel
Ventura, Gregory
Merryweather, Kevin Collins,
Rhett Russo, Peter Cornell.
Façade Consultant: Hugh
Dutton Associates
**• National Library
of France**
Bernard Tschumi,
Luca Merlini, Robert
Young, Koichi Yasuda,
Mark Haukos, Frazer
Gardiner, Jean-Pierre
de l'Or, Ann Krsul,
Phillippe Gavin,
Jean-François Erhel
Consultant: Peter Rice,
Hugh Dutton (RFR)
**• Center for Art and
Media, ZKM**
Bernard Tschumi, Mark
Haukos, Koichi Yasuda,
Jakob Lehrecke, Jean-
Pierre de l'Or, Robert
Young, Midori Yasuda,
Philippe Gavin
• Glass Video Gallery
Bernard Tschumi, Mark
Haukos, Robert Young
• The Hague Villa
Bernard Tschumi, Tom
Kowalski, Mark Haukos,
François Gillet, Therese
Erngaard, Robert Young.
Consultant: Hugh Dutton
(RFR)
• Chartres Business Park
Bernard Tschumi,
Véronique Descharrières,
Karen Dogny, Therese
Erngaard, François Gillet,
Mark Haukos, Tom
Kowalski, Robert Young

174

• **Le Fresnoy National Studio for the Contemporary Arts**
Competition: Bernard Tschumi, François Gillet, Mark Haukos, Tom Kowalski, Robert Young, Jim Sullivan; *project*: Bernard Tschumi, Tom Kowalski, Jean-François Erhel, Véronique Descharrières, François Gillet, Yannis Aesopos, Henning Ehrhart, Douglas Gauthier, Vincent Thevenon, Eric Liftin, Robert Moric, Sheri Olsen, Jordan Parnass, Tsuto Sakamoto
Consultants: Tetraserf; Choulet
• **K-Polis Department Store**
Bernard Tschumi, Gregory Merryweather, Niels Roelfs, Ruth Berktold, Tom Kowalski, Mark Haukos, Kevin Collins
• **Alfred Lerner Student Hall, Columbia University**
Bernard Tschumi/Gruzen Samton Associated Architects
Bernard Tschumi Architects: Bernard Tschumi, Tom Kowalski, Kim Starr, Megan Miller, Mark Haukos, Ruth Berktold, Richard Veith, Galia Solomonoff, Yannis Aesopos, Tony Manzo, Peter Cornell, Jordan Parnass, Stacy Norman.
Gruzen Samton Associates: Peter Samton, Tim Schmiderer, David Terenzio, Ken Hutchinson, Jerzy Lesniak, Scott Broaddus, Liane Williams-Liu, Geoff Doban, Nick Lombardo, John Mulling, Niclas Hedin, Cameron Lory, Jo Goldberger
Consultants: Severud;

ARUP; Special Structures Engineering (suspended ramps and glass wall): ARUP with Hugh Dutton (HDA)
• **School of Architecture, Marne-La-Vallée**
Competition: Bernard Tschumi, Kevin Collins, Yannis Aesopos, Véronique Descharrières, Robert Young, Tom Kowalski, Mark Haukos, Stephanie Bayard, Jordan Parnass, Grace Cheung; *project*: New York: Bernard Tschumi, Kevin Collins, Gregory Merryweather, Rhett Russo, Frederick Norman; Paris: Véronique Descharrières, Alex Reid, Cristina Devizzi, Laurane Ponsonnet
Consultants: Façade: Hugh Dutton (HDA); RFR; Choulet; CIAL; Ursula Kurz; SETEC-TP
• **Expansion of The Museum of Modern Art**
Bernard Tschumi, Kevin Collins, Gregory Merryweather, Peter Cornell, Rhett Russo, Frederick Norman, Ruth Berktold, Tom Kowalski, Kim Starr, Jimmy Miyoshi, Tyson Godfrey, John Cleater, Fiona Whitton, Megan Miller
Consultants: ARUP; HDA; Kate Linker; Model: Kennedy Fabrications, New York and BTA New York
• **Rouen Concert Hall and Exhibition Center**
New York: Bernard Tschumi, Kevin Collins, Peter Cornell, Megan Miller, Joel Rutten, Kim Starr, Roderick Villafranca, Robert Holton; *Paris*: Véronique Descharrières, Alex Reid, Cristina Devizzi, Laurane Ponsonnet
Consultants: Façade: Hugh

Dutton (HDA); Technip Seri; 2ème Acte; Cial
• **School of Architecture, Florida International University**
Bernard Tschumi, Anne Save de Beaurecueil, Johanne Riegels Oestergaard, Valentin Bontjes van Beek, William Feuerman, Joel Rutten, Robert Holton, Kim Starr, Peter Cornell, Andrea Day, Roderick Villafranca
Associate Architect: Bruno Elias Associates (BEA).
Consultants: BEA; TLC
• **Urban Glass House of the 21st Century**
Bernard Tschumi, Johanne Riegels Oestergaard, Andrew Vrana, Philippos Photiadis
• **Carnegie Science Center**
Bernard Tschumi, Kim Starr, Jonathan Chace, Anne Save de Beaurecueil, William Feuerman, Robert Holton, Valentin Bontjes van Beek, Joel Rutten, Kate Linker, Liz Kim
• **Museum for African Art**
Competition: Bernard Tschumi, Kim Starr, Anne Save de Beaurecueil, Johanne Riegels Ostergaard, Joel Rutten, Robert Holton, Valentin Bontjes van Beek, Andrea Day, Kate Linker, Liz Kim, Matt Kelley; *project*: Bernard Tschumi, Kim Starr, Jonathan Chace, Joel Rutten, Valentin Bontjes van Beek, Michaela Metcalfe, Allis Chee, Georgia Papadavid
Interiors: Yolande Daniels
Consultants: ARUP; LERA
• **University of Cincinnati Athletic Center**
Bernard Tschumi, Kim Starr, Robert Holton, Phu Hoang, Jonathan Chace, Jane Kim,

Nicolas Martin, Eva Sopeoglou, Thomas Goodwill, Daniel Holguin, Valentin Bontjes van Beek, Michaela Metcalfe, Allis Chee, Joel Aviles, Justin Moore
Associate Architect: Glaserworks
Consultants: ARUP; THP; Heapy Engineering; Human Nature
• **Vacheron Constantin Watch Factory and Headquarters**
Competition: Bernard Tschumi, Joel Rutten, Véronique Descharrières, Jonathan Chace, Robert Holton, Valentin Bontjes van Beek, Kate Linker, Liz Kim; *project*: Bernard Tschumi, Veronique Descharrières, Joel Rutten, Ludovic Ghirardi, Jonathan Chace, Phu Hoang, Nicolas Martin, Jane Kim, Michaela Metcalfe, Allis Chee, Justin Moore, Joel Aviles, Cristina Devizzi, Alex Reid, Matteo Vigano, Jean Jacques Hubert, Antoine Santiard, Yann Brossier
Local Partner: Eric Maria
Consultants: SGI; Enerconom; Scherler
• **Electronic Media Performing Arts Center**
Bernard Tschumi, Anne Save de Beaurecueil, Kim Starr, Valentin Bontjes van Beek, Jonathan Chace, Liz Kim, Thomas Goodwill, Robert Holton, Joel Rutten
• **New Acropolis Museum**
Competition: Bernard Tschumi, Joel Rutten, Jonathan Chace, Anne Save de Beaurecueil, Robert Holton, Valentin Bontjes van Beek, Kate Linker, Liz Kim, Cristina Devizzi, Kriti Siderakis; *project*: Bernard Tschumi,

Joel Rutten, Kim Starr,
Aristotelis Dimitrakopoulos,
Adam Dayem, Jane Kim,
Michaela Metcalfe, Allis
Chee, Georgia Papadavid,
Justin Moore, Joel Aviles
Associate Architects:
Michael Photiadis, ARSY
Consultants: ARUP; ADK;
MMB; MGS
• **Museu de Arte
Contemporânea**
Bernard Tschumi,
Anne Save de Beaurecueil,
Kim Starr, Robert Holton,
Jonathan Chace,
William Feuerman,
Joel Rutten, Valentin
Bontjes van Beek,
Thomas Goodwill,
Kate Linker, Liz Kim

Credits
Book production: Bernard
Tschumi, Jane Kim

Acknowledgements
Special gratitude is due
to Bernard Tschumi for
his constant cooperation
and courtesy, to the staff
of Bernard Tschumi
Architects, and in particular
to Jane Kim.
Thanks are extended to
Caterina Giavotto of Rizzoli
and the staff of Skira,
especially Luca Molinari
and Marco De Michelis,
for their support and
consideration.
Filippo Clericuzio
and Filippo Romano
provided generous
hospitality in Paris and
New York.
This book owes much
to discussions with
Marco Biraghi, Guia
Camerino, Leila Di Giangi
and Luka Skansi, who
facilitated the project in
numerous ways.

Photographic Credits
Xavier Bouchart: p. 47
Robert Cesar: pp. 87; 88;
92 (bottom)
Sophie Chivet: p. 54
Lydia Gould: pp. 101; 103
(top)
Peter Mauss/ESTO: pp. 49;
51; 52; 69; 71; 72; 73;
74; 75; 85; 89; 90; 92 (top);
97; 99 (bottom); 103
(bottom); 104; 105; 113;
115; 117; 125; 127 (top);
128; 129; 130; 132; 133
(top); 154
J.M. Monthiers: pp. 48; 50
Pinkster and Tahl: pp. 78; 81
(top)
Bernard Tschumi: pp. 6; 81
(bottom); 86; 98; 99 (top);
106; 121; 127 (bottom);
131; 133 (bottom)

Front cover image:
Peter Mauss/ ESTO
Back cover image:
J.M. Monthiers